The
TAXMAN
IS WATCHING

The TAXMAN

IS WATCHING

What Every Canadian Taxpayer Needs to Know and Fear

PAUL DIOGUARDI

PHILIPPE DIOGUARDI

Collins

Published by Collins, an imprint of HarperCollins Publishers Ltd.

The information contained in this book is non-technical and meant for general readership. The authors and publisher disclaim all liability for any damages resulting from the application of the information given in this book. In publishing this book, we are not engaged in rendering legal, accounting, or other professional service. If you are contemplating applications to federal or provincial tax amnesty programs, notices of objection, taxpayer relief submissions, or other topics we cover, you should seek specific, updated advice from experienced, legal tax counsel before proceeding.

DioGuardi Tax Law case histories used in the book have been altered to protect lawyer-client confidentiality.

The cartoon on page 23 is by Graham Harrop (harrop 10–21), *www.grahamharrop.com*. Used by permission.

Pages 45–46, excerpt adapted from Tony Van Alphen, "Couple Jailed in Tax Evasion Case," *Toronto Star*, May 1, 2007, C1. Reprinted by permission—Torstar Syndication Services.

HarperCollins books may be purchased for educational, business, or sales promotional use through our Special Markets Department.

HarperCollins Publishers Ltd.
2 Bloor Street East, 20th Floor
Toronto, Ontario, Canada
M4W 1A8

www.harpercollins.ca

Canadian Cataloguing in Publication information is available.

Printed and bound in Canada
WEB   10   9   8   7   6   5   4   3   2   1

CONTENTS

Two tax agents arrived suddenly in our offices with notification that a client was going to be criminally charged for tax evasion. 'He's in the hospital,' I said, 'dying.' I produced a letter from the man's doctor. That didn't stop the tax agents, who said they were determined to make an example of the poor man. I insisted that they get their supervisor on the telephone, and he was equally impervious to the fact that the man would be dead in a month. I told him that if he continued with this prosecution, I would hold a press conference at the client's bedside and expose the tax department as a greedy and heartless beast. The supervisor got very quiet. Then he asked if he could call me back. Ten minutes later he phoned to tell his agents to drop the matter.

—from the DioGuardi Tax Law case files,
as told by Paul DioGuardi, QC

1

YOUR RELATIONSHIP WITH THE CANADA REVENUE AGENCY (AND WHY YOU SHOULD BE VERY AFRAID)

"Tax. *noun* 1. a compulsory financial contribution imposed by a government to raise revenue, levied on income or property, on the prices of goods and services, etc. 2. a heavy demand on something; a strain. [From Old French *taxer*, from Latin *taxare* to appraise, from tangere to touch]"

Source: *Collins Canadian English Dictionary*, 2004.

Any time a drab recycled paper envelope bearing the CRA logo arrives in the mail, how many Canadians can truly say their heart doesn't skip a beat before they open it up to discover the message within?

Is it a Notice of Audit? A reassessment? An objection to a deduction made on your last tax return? Or—good news—acceptance of your return with a statement showing there is no tax owing . . . for now.

Instinctively, Canadians seem to understand that their relationship with the CRA is based principally upon fear. Fear that they have done something wrong. Fear that a small mistake on a tax return gone by will one day come back to haunt them. Fear that the Agency will continue to take more of their money before they even see it.

And we should be very afraid. Every taxpayer—even the most conscientious, T4-salaried, always-file-on-time Canadian—stands in danger of the Agency's scrutiny. It could be in the form of a reassessment, or even worse, an audit. Once the CRA has turned its eye on you, it will treat you as if you were already guilty of the tax transgression it is determined to prove you have committed.

Why, then, when that drab envelope arrives in the mailbox, do so many Canadians insist on dealing with the CRA as a trusted friend?

We Canadians are amazingly accepting of our heavy burden of tax. The majority of us say we believe that paying taxes is a social responsibility—the price we willingly accept for health care, for highways, for public safety, and social order. "Peace, order, and good government" is our national mantra.

We think that most of us do pay our taxes, and that we pay them on time. And we are incredibly smug in our belief that, in return for our dutiful acceptance of our taxes, we will be rewarded with the respect and gratitude of the tax authorities. Only non-filers, non-payers, and cheaters have reason to be wary of the CRA.

Nothing could be further from the truth!

Our American neighbours have always had a healthy fear of the Internal Revenue Service—affectionately known the world over as the IRS. Perhaps this began with the case of Al Capone who, despite his status as Public Enemy #1, was able to elude criminal charges until the IRS used the results of a lifestyle audit to indict him for not paying income tax.

Capone allegedly remarked that tax laws were a joke because "the government can't collect legal taxes on illegal money." Unfortunately, he was unaware that the tax laws make no distinction on how income is earned. Even the proceeds of crime are subject to tax. Capone was convicted of tax evasion in 1931 and served 11 in years in prison.

Since Capone, the IRS has become notorious for its draconian pursuit of tax evaders, and a long list of high-profile Americans have been prosecuted for cheating on their taxes. Some highlights include:

Leona Helmsley: After claiming some $2.6 million worth of phony business expenses, the "Queen of Mean" was found guilty of tax fraud in 1992 and spent four years in prison. She was reputed to have boasted, "Only the little people pay taxes."

Spiro Agnew: In 1973, while serving as vice-president to Richard Nixon, he was charged with tax evasion and money laundering. He pleaded no contest to the charges, agreed to resign, and received three years' probation and a $10,000 fine.

Joseph Nunan: The IRS commissioner from 1944–47 was charged in 1952 with criminal tax evasion for failing to report $1,800 in winnings from a bet that Harry Truman would win the presidential election.

Dennis Kozlowski: The former CEO of Tyco bought $13 million worth of paintings in 1992 for his Manhattan apartment. He tried to avoid paying sales tax by making it appear as if they were shipped out of state. An indictment for tax evasion prompted his resignation from Tyco. He is currently serving a 25-year sentence for other dubious business practices.

Willie Nelson: In 1990, the country music singer received a bill from the IRS for $16.7 million in back taxes. The IRS confiscated and auctioned off all his assets to pay the arrears. Ironically, Nelson later became an advertising spokesperson for H&R Block.

Richard Hatch: Famous for being the first winner of the popular reality TV show *Survivor,* Hatch neglected to pay taxes on his $1 million grand prize. He was convicted in 2006 of tax evasion and sentenced to 51 months in prison, plus three years of supervised release after serving his sentence.

Wesley Snipes: The actor ran into trouble in 2006 when the government accused him of failing to file tax returns for the years 1999 through 2004. He pleaded not guilty on Dec. 8, 2006, and was released on a $1 million bond. If convicted, Snipes could face up to 16 years in prison and substantial fines.

These are high-profile convictions, but there are thousands upon thousands of real-life scenarios that see families evicted from their homes, ordinary people reduced to penury, and tax debtors so debilitated with dread that their job performance suffers, their personal lives fall apart, and, in the case of military personnel, they may be prohibited from being deployed for duty abroad in an active war zone.

The IRS has gone out of its way to create a "brand personality" based on fear and intimidation, and its frightening powers are deeply imbedded in the American psyche.

Strangely, Canadians do not mirror these feelings in our relationships with our own federal tax authority.

Ask a Canadian to name a high-profile Canadian tax-evasion case, and you'll likely get a blank stare. A few of the well-read may mumble about Lord Black of Crossharbour—Conrad to his Bay Street colleagues—but they'll quickly refer that case back to issues with the IRS. Why? Because in Canada, we don't think of the Agency as the enemy. We don't believe that our tax authorities would ever do anything to harm us. In fact, most Canadians are entirely misinformed about the powers and governing mission of the CRA.

Take this quick quiz to see how much you really understand about what the CRA can and can't do. The questions themselves will begin to raise doubts about the benign relationship you think Canadians have with the CRA. The answers may keep you up at night.

TAXMAN TRUE OR FALSE?

- Nobody ever goes to jail for not filing a tax return. (It's just a scare tactic to get people to pay up.)
  FALSE. People do go to jail. Sentences are a maximum of two years for each summary conviction, and up to five years for each conviction on indictment. Typically, you face a different charge for each tax year involved and for each breach of the Income Tax Act, which can result in multiple convictions and multiple jail sentences to be served consecutively. It can add up to serious jail time.

- If The CRA hasn't questioned your return after four years, you got away with it.
  FALSE. If there is evidence of fraud or misrepresentation of income, the Agency can come after you at any time for any tax year.

- Transfer your assets into your spouse's name and the CRA won't be able to take anything.
  FALSE. If the transfer of assets is made after there is tax owing, your spouse will share your responsibility for paying the tax, up to the fair market value of the assets he or she received from you.

- You should always feel comfortable talking to the CRA on your own because they work for the government and they're on your side.

FALSE. The CRA is the government's collection agency, with police powers to investigate you and recommend charging you with offences against the tax code. Anything you tell them can be used against you in tax court or criminal court.

- The CRA has the power to order your bank to provide records of your financial transactions without your permission.
  TRUE. The Income Tax Act gives the Agency the power to require information about you from any source it chooses. Banks and credit card companies, among others, are required by law to provide records of your transactions if so requested by the CRA. There is no requirement to inform you or seek your permission.

- The CRA is under no obligation to notify you that a lien has been registered against your home or other property.
  TRUE. In the collection of tax—and especially if there is concern that you may sell or mortgage your property in an attempt to avoid payment of tax—the CRA has the power to seize assets and register a lien against real property without notifying you.

- The CRA has a special 1-800 number that people can call to snitch on suspected tax evaders.
  TRUE. The CRA encourages people to report tax evaders by calling their local tax services office. Reports may be made anonymously.

- The CRA makes public the names and sentencing details of convicted tax evaders.
  TRUE. The CRA issues press releases detailing the names and offences of convicted tax evaders. These can be found in the media room on the CRA website under "Convictions." The

stories are often picked up by newspapers and radio newsrooms and reported publicly.

How did you do? The more answers you got right, the healthier your respect for the Agency.

TAXPAYER DO'S AND DON'TS

- **Don't** think the Agency will never worry about you. You can be on the CRA's radar without even knowing it. The federal tax authorities already monitor tax evasion suspects with "lifestyle" or "net-worth" audits that scrutinize bank accounts and credit card transactions, in search of anomalies between income reported and income spent. And when they ask the bank to hand over your records, the bank, by law, is obliged to do so.

- **Don't** treat tax evasion as a mildly embarrassing social faux pas. You can go to jail for up to two years on summary conviction for *one* count of tax evasion. If the Crown elects to proceed by indictment, the sentence is a maximum of five years. If you are convicted of multiple counts of tax evasion, the sentences could be imposed consecutively, condemning you to several years of incarceration. On top of that, there would be criminal fines ranging from no less than 100% of the tax evaded to a maximum penalty of 200% of the tax evaded. And you still have to pay the tax owing, with interest. Even if you don't go to jail, you can be financially ruined, to say nothing of the social stigma of having your name made public.

- **Don't** trust the CRA to honour a verbal deal. An agent of the tax department is not legally bound to honour a verbal commitment to you regarding protection from prosecution or settlement of a tax issue. Only an experienced tax lawyer can negotiate a legally-binding settlement on your behalf. You wouldn't go into court without defence counsel. Don't attempt to negotiate with the CRA without the same legal protection.

- **Do** seek legal counsel to clean up your tax evasion before the tax agency comes looking for you. Anybody can become a tax evader—knowingly or by innocent oversight. But it is easier to negotiate a settlement of your outstanding tax liability when the CRA doesn't know your name. So if you've been avoiding your legal obligations, clean up your act now with a lawyer-negotiated tax amnesty. You'll be protected from criminal prosecution and financial penalties, and in some cases you may even be granted a waiver of interest or not taxed for some of the years owing.

- **Do** seek the counsel of an appropriately experienced tax lawyer when you run into trouble with the CRA. You could be in a dispute over your tax assessment; or have a large tax bill that you can't afford to pay; or want to protect your assets with a tax-compliant offshore structure (yes, it can be done legally); or, worst-case scenario, you may already be under investigation and be facing charges in criminal court. Whatever the problem, you are entitled to protect your rights as a citizen and as a taxpayer by seeking legal counsel. Don't expect your accountant, the helpful associate at the local tax preparation franchise, or the family member who studied accounting at school to be able to help you talk your way out of the problem. Legal matters need legal assistance, and once you're in trouble with the CRA, it's legal.

- **Don't** be afraid to fight back! As a taxpayer, you have the right to defend your position, or dispute the opinion of the tax authorities. But you have to know how to do it. The following chapters will provide you with the insights and information you need to talk back to the CRA. Think of this as a taxpayer's prescription—a suite of legal remedies to help you cure your tax problems without nasty side effects.

2

MEET THE AGENCY

 Introducing a simplified tax return for all Canadians:

1. How much money did you earn? $ _____

2. Send it all to us. And have a nice day.

Let us introduce you to the CRA and its true purpose.

Originally called the Department of National Revenue, Canada's federal tax authority has changed its name several times and is now called the Canada Revenue Agency. For brevity, we will refer to this entity as the CRA or the Agency.

The next section, "A Tax Agency Who's Who," outlines the CRA's current organizational structure.

A TAX AGENCY WHO'S WHO

The CRA reports to the **Minister of National Revenue,** who is, in turn, accountable to Parliament for all the CRA's activities.

A **Board of Management,** consisting of 15 members, oversees the organization and management of the CRA. It does not have the authority to administer and enforce legislation or to access confidential client information.

The bureaucrat in charge of the Agency on a day-to-day basis is the **Commissioner,** who is responsible for the administration and enforcement of the Income Tax and Excise Tax acts.

Reporting to the Commissioner is a team of **Assistant Commissioners,** who manage the various departments of the CRA. Most taxpayers will be involved with only the Agency's **Assessment and Benefits Services, Compliance Programs,** and—if they are ever brave enough to stand up to the Agency—**Appeals.**

The **"tax police"**—the Agency's undercover "detectives" who, in their never-ending search for more tax dollars, stage covert operations to gather evidence for the laying of criminal charges—work for **Compliance Programs.** Their performance is key to the achievement of the fiscal targets described in this chapter. Later in this book you will read more about initiatives of the "tax police," including lifestyle audits, net-worth assessments, and criminal investigations.

Equally dangerous, although they initially seem quite benign, are the people who work in **Assessment and Benefits.** They review your tax return, and score it to determine if anything you have declared—or not declared—warrants deeper investigation. (For more on scoring, see Chapter 3.) If you don't pass muster, they hand your file over to the "tax police."

Employees of **Taxpayer Services and Debt Management** are the people who, like the medieval Sheriff of Nottingham in the tale of Robin Hood, have the authority to enforce payment of your assessed tax owing by freezing your bank accounts, placing liens against your home, and seizing other assets.

The CRA's auditors are part of **Compliance Programs**. More than 5,500 people work full-time in the Audit Department, accounting for more than 12% of the total CRA workforce. If, in the course of an audit, evidence of deliberate deception is discovered, the auditors will invite the "tax police" to begin a separate investigation. This may lead to criminal prosecution, which, if successful, brings more tax dollars into the CRA coffers in the form of penalties and interest.

Appeals exists to provide a channel for the taxpayer to dispute or refute a tax assessment, or, in cases of personal and financial hardship, request some form of tax relief. One would think this division would have the taxpayer's well-being as its greatest consideration. Not so. When dealing with Appeals, the onus is entirely on the taxpayer to disprove the validity of the tax assessment. In the majority of cases, the Appeals officer rules in favour of the CRA. But why would this be otherwise? The Appeals officer works for the CRA, and is most interested in the bottom line results of the Agency's endeavours.

When faced with such odds, the taxpayer seeking redress must go outside the auspices of the CRA and appeal to a higher authority—the **Tax Court of Canada**, which is an independent court of law charged with ruling on disputes between taxpayers and tax authorities.

When dealing with Appeals, the onus is entirely on the taxpayer to disprove the validity of the tax assessment. In the majority of cases, the Appeals officer rules in favour of the CRA.

VITAL STATISTICS

The CRA is charged with administering and enforcing Canada's many tax laws, which are revised every time our legislators devise and pass into law new ways to demand our money. Here are some pertinent facts and figures about the CRA:

Tax returns processed annually

29 million income tax returns, including:
- 25 million individual
- 1.6 million corporate
- 400,000 trust
- 78,000 charity
- 3 million GST/HST returns (excluding Quebec, which administers the GST in that province on behalf of the CRA)

Revenue collected annually

$330 billion—about $1.3 billion for every working day of the year. That total includes (in numbers rounded to the closest billion):
- $52 billion in taxes levied by the provinces, territories, and First Nations
- $17 billion in Employment Insurance (EI) premiums
- $30 billion on behalf of the Canada Pension Plan (CPP)

Number of employees

Over 44,000 full-time across Canada, with 5,350 for audit program staffing alone:
- 3,000 for small- and medium-business income tax
- 1,500 for GST and HST
- 250 for medium-enterprise income tax

- 500 for Office Audit
- 750 for non-registrants and non-filers

Like any business unit within a mega corporation, the CRA is expected to deliver a measurable return on the bottom line to its parent company, the Government of Canada. To that end, here are some of the Agency's strategic imperatives and revenue targets, based upon recently available published reports.

CRA CORPORATE BUSINESS PLAN PRIORITIES
(FOR TAX YEARS 2007-2008 TO 2009-2010)

- Increase focus on aggressive tax planning, in particular the abusive use of international transactions and tax havens
- Continue to combat the underground economy, and GST/HST fraud
- Enhance programs to address interprovincial tax avoidance and provincial income allocation
- Continue development and implementation of a compliance communications strategy action plan that uses communications to promote compliance
- Improve the administration of the Voluntary Disclosures Program (VDP)

Can you see the emerging trend? Even in the statements of "corporate" business objectives, the focus is on targeting segments of the taxpayer base for increased investigation in the Agency's relentless pursuit of more tax dollars. There is also a baseline assumption that cheating is the norm. It's ironic, given that these aggressive compliance measures are directed against the same people who, as citizens of Canada, are the shareholders in and beneficiaries of the financial success of the parent corporation—the Government of Canada.

A quick overview of the CRA's spending projections shows the lion's share of funding directed toward tax compliance and enforcement programs.

CRA PLANNED SPENDING BY PROGRAM

Program Activities Planned per Year for the Tax Years 2006-2007 through 2008-2009 (shown in thousands of dollars)

Client Assistance	309,857
Assessment of Returns and Payments Processing	756,232
Filing and Remittance Compliance	613,743
Reporting Compliance	1,094,507
Appeals	128,333

The allotment for Filing and Remittance Compliance (otherwise known as payment of the tax bill) is almost double the amount earmarked for services that help taxpayers with the complex and onerous process of tax filing. Reporting Compliance, which refers to the tax evaders who don't file, or don't honestly report all their income, is more than triple the client assistance budget.

Given these figures, there's no mistaking the Agency's business priorities.

STACKED IN THE CRA'S FAVOUR

The laws of the land give the CRA an exceptionally wide range of powers and privileges. The deck is heavily stacked in its favour from the outset.

According to the Income Tax Act, taxpayers must disclose their income annually and estimate the tax payable according to guidelines provided by the tax agency each year. Failure to do so accurately, and in a timely manner, can result in criminal prosecution.

Here are the relevant excerpts from the Income Tax Act:

Income Tax Act, Section 238(1)
- Failure to file return at required time and in required manner
- Failure to deduct or withhold tax
- Failure to keep proper books and records

Penalty: On summary conviction, a fine from $1,000 to $25,000 and imprisonment for up to 12 months.

Income Tax Act, Section 239(1)(2)
- Making false or deceptive statements in documents
- Alteration, falsification, or destruction of accounting books or records to evade payment of taxes
- Wilful evasion or attempt to evade payment of taxes

Penalty: On summary conviction, a fine of from 50% to 200% of tax sought to be evaded, and imprisonment for up to two years. If by indictment, a fine of from 100% to 200% of tax sought to be evaded, and imprisonment for up to five years.

The Agency operates as the Government of Canada's collection agency. It has policelike powers to investigate suspected violations; search and seize taxpayer records; enforce collection of tax owing; freeze, seize, or encumber taxpayer assets in lieu of collection; and, through the Department of Justice, prosecute taxpayers in criminal court. In addition, the CRA has the right to demand a full disclosure of your financial history and transactions from your bank without your knowledge or permission. When the Agency demands any of the above information, your bank, your accountant, your employer, your spouse—whoever is asked—is compelled by law to comply.

It doesn't sound like a very friendly relationship. Yet the CRA has, in recent years, gone out of its way to present a very approachable face to Canadian taxpayers, whom it refers to as its "clients." Call the CRA and, typically, you will speak with a very pleasant individual who appears sympathetic and understanding of your needs—much like a loans officer at your bank.

When the Agency demands information, your bank, your accountant, your employer, your spouse—whoever is asked—is compelled by law to comply.

This is what we call the "civil" face of the Agency. But like the Roman god Janus, the CRA has an opposite face and attitude that approaches every taxpayer as an unproven tax evader. Once the Agency's eye is upon you, every conversation, every interaction is focused on gathering evidence to extract more tax and/or civil penalties from you and, if warranted, build a case for criminal prosecution. CRA agents are trained to believe that you, the taxpayer, have something to hide. They will try to win your confidence with their civil face, encouraging you to voluntarily share information about yourself and your finances so that what you say can be used as evidence against you.

You most likely will have no idea that you are under criminal investigation until your case is passed over to the Department of Justice for prosecution. By then it is too late to protect yourself. The evidence you so willingly revealed to the "nice person from the tax department" now forms the basis of the case against you.

It's difficult for a taxpayer to determine when the questions stop being routine and start becoming dangerous. The safest rule-of-thumb is to assume from the outset that the Agency is not on your side. At the first sign of any investigative action, seek the advice of an experienced tax lawyer.

Why, then, do we persist in thinking the CRA is our friend?

Much of this insight is probably new and distressing to the average Canadian taxpayer. It's hardly surprising given the benign image the CRA works so hard to make us believe.

In the Agency's *Corporate Business Plan* for the tax years 2007–2008 to 2009–2010, it speaks of its commitment to "implement a communications strategy that emphasizes the image of the CRA as a responsive service provider and promotes the CRA's contribution to the efficiency of government and the well-being of Canadians."

As part of this strategy, in May 2007 the CRA presented, with great fanfare, a new and improved Taxpayer Bill of Rights, offering 15 articles for the protection of taxpayers in general, plus a new five-article commitment to small businesses. The Agency also created the new role of Taxpayers' Ombudsman to better "protect" the rights of the taxpayer.

TAXPAYER BILL OF RIGHTS

- You have the right to receive entitlements and to pay no more and no less than what is required by law.
- You have the right to service in both official languages.
- You have the right to privacy and confidentiality.
- You have the right to a formal review and a subsequent appeal.
- You have the right to be treated professionally, courteously, and fairly.
- You have the right to complete, accurate, clear, and timely information.
- You have the right, as an individual, not to pay income tax amounts in dispute before you have had an impartial review.
- You have the right to have the law applied consistently.
- You have the right to lodge a service complaint and to be provided with an explanation of our findings.
- You have the right to have the costs of compliance taken into account when administering tax legislation.
- You have the right to expect us to be accountable.
- You have the right to relief from penalties and interest under tax legislation because of extraordinary circumstances.
- You have the right to expect us to publish our service standards and report annually.
- You have the right to expect us to warn you about questionable tax schemes in a timely manner.
- You have the right to be represented by a person of your choice.

While this bill is presented as a statement of rights, the content reads as a service manifesto. The Agency studiously does not mention your Charter right not to be forced to incriminate yourself. Nor does it mention that, if you choose to withhold tax until the outcome of your dispute or appeal is resolved, you will nonetheless be charged penalties and interest accruing from the day the alleged tax was due. Moreover, as specified in the supporting text for Article 7, "in certain circumstances that are specified in the legislation, the CRA can exercise its authority to take collection action even though an objection or appeal has been filed." By this, the Agency means that it can freeze or seize assets in advance of the resolution of your tax case if it feels that you may do something to make your assets unavailable for seizure.

This doesn't sound so taxpayer-friendly after all.

As for the creation of a Taxpayers' Ombudsman, read the official details and judge for yourself:

> The Minister of National Revenue has established the position of Taxpayers' Ombudsman to enhance the Canada Revenue Agency's (CRA) accountability and service to the public and to provide the people it serves with renewed assurance that they will be treated fairly, equitably, and with respect.
>
> The Taxpayers' Ombudsman is an independent and impartial officer who will operate at arm's length from the CRA and report to the Minister of National Revenue.
>
> The Taxpayers' Ombudsman will be charged with reviewing service-related complaints about the CRA and upholding the Taxpayer Bill of Rights with regard to service matters. The Ombudsman will be the final level of review in the CRA complaint resolution process, including the CRA Service Complaints program.

We wonder how impartial this Ombudsman (who at the time of this book's writing had yet to be appointed by the government of the day) can be when he or she will report directly to the Minister of National Revenue—the government official who has responsibility for the performance (read: revenue generation capability) of the CRA. Moreover, it clearly states that the Ombudsman has authority to mitigate the taxpayer experience only in terms of service. The Ombudsman has no ability to protect the taxpayer from a tax agency that can, at times, be far too diligent in its pursuit of tax dollars.

As one columnist in a national newspaper commented:

> It's tempting to dismiss the whole initiative as a PR exercise. . . . It's also unclear whether the objective is to make the agency more feared—like its American counterpart, the IRS—or less feared. Presumably, the latter, since [Minister of National Revenue] Skelton said one goal was to make the CRA more 'user-friendly.'

THE REAL DEAL

Federal and provincial governments operate on the assumption that a large percentage of our income can be taken from us by them as their right. We are told that taxation is the price of civilization, and in a sense this is true. The real question is the level of taxation. How much is enough? How much is too much? Government rapacity has gotten out of hand, to the extent that Canadians are now subjected to a minimum of 51 types of tax. If you live in Ontario, the introduction of the health tax makes it 52 and counting.

This litany of tax upon tax confirms the public suspicion that our tax system is unfair. Few understand that the Agency doesn't have to be fair. Tax laws are strictly interpreted by the courts. The law doesn't require fairness.

Tax officials have the power, without giving any notice, to get a secret judgment in the federal court allowing them to seize your assets, often the family home. They can also conduct a search and seizure in your home, place of business, or elsewhere while being assisted, ostensibly to "keep the peace," by police officers or, if necessary, the RCMP. This includes "sneak and peek" searches, when authorized by a warrant, where the target is not aware the tax authorities have entered a premises surreptitiously and copied documents, or noted locations of items to be seized at a later time.

 Canadians are now subjected to a minimum of 51 types of tax. If you live in Ontario, the introduction of the health tax makes it 52 and counting.

Knowing all this, it is little wonder that, of all the nouns in the English lexicon, none causes more angst and despair than the word *tax*. It's the demand that never goes away. No sooner do you settle accounts with the CRA for one year than the tax owing for the next year is presented for payment. The harder you work, the more tax you pay. If you don't pay in full by the prescribed deadline, the CRA sweetens its take by adding penalties and daily interest. All you, the taxpayer, can do is understand the dangers and do what you can to protect yourself from unfair persecution. Legal avenues are available to uphold your rights as a taxpayer.

3

TRACKING TAX

In the eyes of the Agency, there is no such thing as an honest taxpayer.

In Chapter 1 we established that the CRA is driven by two overarching objectives: to collect as much revenue as possible; and to assess as much tax as is possible under the provisions of the Income Tax Act.

Here we will examine the lengths to which the Agency will go to achieve those objectives.

Like the Ancient Greek skeptic Diogenes, who took a torch in full daylight and went searching for an honest man—but found only rascals and scoundrels—the Agency shines a torch on every tax return to spotlight the cheaters and evaders.

Every fall, the CRA's state-of-the-art "matching program" systematically scans all personal income tax returns and matches the information reported on your return with information reported by employers, financial institutions, business partners, and any other third parties. The system also compares your tax return to that of your spouse or common-law partner. If the tallies don't match, you're suddenly a candidate for the Agency's Most Wanted list.

MATCHING TAX—THE CRA'S T4 INCOME SLIP MATCHING PROGRAM

When a discrepancy is identified, the system calculates how much additional income tax would be owed if the discrepancy were corrected. If your score is high enough—meaning if you would owe enough additional tax to warrant the effort and expense of the Agency coming after you—then your return is passed on for further review. The nature and source of the unreported income determines what type of enforcement action will be taken. You may simply be reassessed and sent a new tax bill. Or you may be flagged for audit. Or you may become the subject of a criminal investigation.

 Every fall, the CRA's state-of-the-art "matching program" compares your tax return to that of your spouse or common-law partner.

Imagine the dismay of a Manitoba teenager who filed her first tax return in April 2007. She expected to net a return of a few hundred dollars—welcome spending money for the coming school year. Instead, the CRA sent her an assessment for $20,000, and gave her two weeks to pay. A manager at the Canada Revenue grudgingly admitted that "the assessors might have gotten the student's paperwork wrong."

"Matching" is merely stage-one triage when compared to the other sources available to the Agency. Here's a list of different sources of information that are easily available to them.

Government Records

Information may be obtained from various official records such as:
- sale and transfer of property
- mortgages and discharges
- court actions (especially divorce litigation)
- judgments, garnishments, and other liens
- conditional sales contracts
- births, deaths, marriages, and divorces
- change of name
- auto licences, transfers, and sales of vehicles
- drivers' licences
- hunting and fishing licences
- occupancy and business permit licences
- building and other permits
- police records of arrests and convictions
- court records of civil and criminal cases

- registration of corporations and annual corporate reports
- registration of non-corporate business entities
- school and voter registrations
- professional registrations
- provincial (Quebec) income tax returns
- personal property tax returns
- real estate property tax payments
- inheritance information
- wills
- welfare agency records
- Workers' Compensation files
- civil service applications

Business, Financial, Professional, and Education Records

Businesses and organizations maintain records of their dealings with individuals or corporations. These often include financial transactions, personal identification or licencing data, and a variety of other information that is valuable to the Agency.

Investigative Databases

Computer databases are available on the Internet to tax agents looking for information on potential targets. Netscape's Net Directory and other search engines provide nationwide name search capability. There are databases of alumni associations, people holding professional licences, society memberships, club memberships, business customers, and subscribers to various services. A large number of other organizations maintain lists that allow parties to contact people with similar interests, or those who are in search of business or professional relationships. The Agency can use these lists to provide a fast, inexpensive means of obtaining useful leads. The Agency also has access to

LexisNexis, a legal reporting service, which provides the latest information on published legal decisions across the country. These can be a gold mine of information on possible tax evasion.

An additional source of information is the database marketing industry, which is replete with companies that specialize in assembling, for a fee, data on everyone in the country. Information about you, where you shop, what you buy, how many times a year you travel abroad, how many times you eat out . . . It can all be sliced, diced, and served any way the CRA wants it. And, unlike the commercial users of these services who pay hefty fees for access to this data, the CRA can demand it for free.

Informants

Some tax cases under investigation by the Agency cannot be successfully completed unless an informant is used to help acquire evidence of tax evasion. In the US, the IRS pays a reward to informants. Payment is not yet legal in Canada, but the Agency has its own snitch line that friends, neighbours, competitors, ex-spouses, jilted lovers, and anyone else with a grudge can call to "suggest" that the CRA investigate your financial activities.

WHY THE AGENCY IS WATCHING SO CLOSELY

Most Canadians say that they agree with the statement, engraved in stone at the top of the IRS headquarters, that "taxes are what we pay for a civilized society." However, according to comparative benchmark studies, non-compliance with tax reporting has grown by 88% since 1997.

Clearly, many ordinary people feel that it's "okay" to hide a little income here and there. With our personal and corporate tax rates adding up to one of the highest in the world, who can blame a taxpayer for deciding enough is enough and making his or her own decision about when not to declare a portion of income?

The CRA can—and does. That's why the Agency automatically assumes that every taxpayer has something to hide. Even in the routine pursuit of tax assessment and collection, CRA agents are actively on the lookout for tax evasion. Their favourite target? You and me. Otherwise known as "the little guys."

It is normal for "the little guy" to simply shrug off the Agency's enforcement drive. The common refrain is, "I'm just an ordinary person and only cheat a bit on my taxes, so why would the 'tax police' bother with me?"

Here's why: Put together, all the ordinary, everyday tax cheaters represent a huge amount of uncollected tax. The 2004 Report of the Auditor General cites that the Small and Medium Enterprise (SME) Audit Program in 2002–2003 collected some $1.7 billion from non-registrants and non-filers. This figure does not include the revenue generated from audits and reassessments of these business categories, which totals a further $2.05 billion.

It is certainly well worth the Agency's effort to go after these little fish. Moreover, the small folk tend to be easier prey, because individuals and small business owners are less likely to have—or be able to afford—an army of lawyers at their command.

Put together, all the ordinary, everyday tax cheaters represent a huge amount of uncollected tax.

Big or small, tax evasion is so rampant that the Agency is aggressively, and increasingly, pursuing both the big players and the ordinary "little guys," prosecuting and making public examples of them, in the hope that others will think twice about evading taxes.

Here's a real-life example of a "little fish" who was caught in the Agency's net, not because a large amount of tax was owed, but for the simple crime—and it is indeed a crime—of not filing tax returns.

THE CASE OF THE FRAZZLED HAIRDRESSER

When Suzie was still in her twenties, she opened a hairdressing salon and incorporated her business. It didn't make any money and eventually it went under. She just let the whole matter drop and, over the course of several years, ignored repeated notices from the Ministry of Finance to file corporate tax returns for the defunct business. Then the police arrived at her door with a subpoena to appear in criminal court. Suzie was being criminally charged for failure to file corporate tax returns.

Suzie and her husband were dumbfounded. There was no income in the business. There was no tax due. How could she be evading taxes? Who knew she was supposed to file tax returns for a business that had no revenue?

"I'm not a criminal," Suzie sobbed. Clearly Suzie had not received—or had not sought—appropriate tax advice.

As her legal counsel, we called the Ministry of Finance to investigate and were told that they were cracking down on corporate non-filers. "Too many people are ignoring us," they said. "We have decided that criminal prosecution is the only way to make these small businesses compliant. We'll see you in court!" And that was the end of the phone call.

After two appearances in criminal court, and filing the missing corporate tax returns (which, upon careful review, did indeed show zero taxable income), we were able to negotiate the criminal charges being withdrawn. But Suzie was still liable to pay penalties for non-filing. The Agency lost the big prize—a criminal conviction—but still came out trumps with cash in hand.

THE AGENCY TARGETS SMALL-TIME TAX SERVICE PROVIDERS

Determined to stop the increasing rise in tax fraud, the Agency will continue to scrutinize hundreds of thousands of tax returns every year, and prosecute those it catches in the act of tax fraud.

Key targets are unscrupulous tax preparers, and their clients. These self-styled accountants usually have little or no formal training, and are unlikely to be accredited accounting professionals with Chartered Accountant (CA) or certified accountant (CMA, CGA) credentials. They often counsel their clients into "grey" or "aggressive" accounting practices, with the offhand reassurance that "the taxman will never notice. And if he does, we'll just say it was a mistake." Competition for tax preparation business is so fierce that some tax preparers only win business based on their ability to help the taxpayer pay less tax and/or get a larger refund.

What you, the taxpayer, must understand is that *you* are the one who signs your tax return. Therefore *you* are legally responsible for all the statements and claims made on your return. If the Agency finds evidence of cheating, either by you or your tax preparer, it will come after you first—and then go after your tax preparer, who can also be convicted for counselling tax evasion.

This is where a deeper danger lies. Regardless of whether or not a tax preparer is under investigation and eventually charged, typically the Agency will look at the tax returns for all his or her clients. All clients are then at risk of investigation, audit, and reassessment, and will be liable for interest and penalties on taxes that should have been paid. If the investigation includes several years of returns—and if the Agency finds evidence of fraud or misrepresentation—there is no limit to the number of years the CRA can go back and revisit. The penalties and interest can add up to enormous sums, even if the CRA chooses to forgo criminal prosecution.

 If the Agency finds evidence of cheating, either by you or your tax preparer, it will come after you first.

Your best protection is to be careful in your choice of tax preparation assistance. Certified professionals like Chartered Accountants (CA), Certified Management Accountants (CMA), or Certified General Accountants (CGA) are subject to regulatory authorities and are bound by a code of professional conduct that offers you assurance that their accounting practices are tax compliant and trustworthy. Be wary of all others.

THE AGENCY IS ALWAYS WATCHING THE SELF-EMPLOYED

If you work for yourself you probably already are on the CRA's radar in one way or another. Self-employed workers and small-business owners are responsible for self-reporting their income and remitting their taxes. GST is also involved unless the total annual income is less than $30,000. Remember Suzie? It's a classic scenario that the self-employed will have to use the income they earn throughout the year to survive. Unless they are particularly disciplined, probably there is not enough money sitting in the bank to pay the Agency when tax time rolls around each year. The temptation is huge to just not file, or to cheat on the numbers so that the tax bill becomes affordable.

A self-employed small business owner is much more likely to be targeted for audit than the T4-salaried employee. Expect the Agency also to pay much more attention to self-employed subcontractors. The Agency uses a complicated test to determine if a person is an independent contractor or an employee. If it is determined that a contracted individual is really an employee, both the employer and the employee will face stiff penalties.

A self-employed small business owner is much more likely to be targeted for audit than the T4-salaried employee.

You can, of course, appeal a negative decision to higher authorities. The tax court will examine the nature and degree of control over the person alleged to be an independent contractor. They also consider if the work done is integral to the business or only accessory to it. In the latter situation, the taxpayer will be an independent contractor. There is also an economic reality test. The bottom line is that a court will review all the facts of the relationship in detail, and the results will vary from case to case.

If you are not sure where your working relationship falls, consult a certified tax professional or a tax lawyer.

THE AGENCY'S NEW SECRET WEAPONS: ACCOUNTANTS AND BANKERS

Stepping up the assault on non-compliant taxpayers, the CRA is increasing the pressure on accountants, bankers, and financial advisers to reveal information about clients suspected of being tax evaders. Third-party liability penalties are very high, and are a strong incentive for your accountant or adviser to turn you in to the Agency. If you are prosecuted for tax evasion, chances are good that your accountant will be the CRA's star witness in court.

This third-party liability is also extended to bankers, stockbrokers, and other financial advisers. The bottom line: all financial service providers, whether they like it or not, are aligned with the Agency and, in effect, have become legislated government informants. The taxpayer, however, generally is unaware that sharing secrets with accountants, financial advisers, and bankers has become so risky.

ELECTRONIC BANKING: A WINDOW INTO THE TAX EVADER'S SOUL

In today's computerized world, there's no way you can avoid having your spending habits registered somewhere. Every time you use a credit card, debit, or discount card, the information finds its way into a database. Records of your spending habits can be linked to your financial history. It is easy for the CRA to get information from these databases on where you travel, what restaurants you dine at, the type of car you drive, what you buy, and with whom you do business. This is the Agency's preferred weapon in a secret lifestyle assessment. Your bank and your credit card providers are obliged to provide this information to the Agency upon request, without notifying you.

You can be in for a nasty surprise if your spending doesn't tally with the Agency's records of the taxable income you declared was earned each year.

This information is used as a tip to begin investigating individuals who have failed to file or have evaded taxes. Electronic lifestyle audits can be started using financial information already in circulation. Here, your privacy rights are not very effective because when you signed your credit card agreement, you most likely traded them off to merchants for some monetary advantage, such as a lower interest rate, frequent flyer points, or bonus rewards.

In a letter to a reporter in the *Ottawa Citizen* in January 2007, the Federal Privacy Commissioner stated that the Privacy Act contains nothing that can compel government to remedy any deficiencies in the way it collects, uses, and discloses personal information. When the Agency goes on a fishing expedition, so much for any privacy rights you thought you had!

EVEN IN CYBERSPACE, THE AGENCY IS WATCHING

The CRA has recently added a digital agent to the team. It's a cyberbot program, or digital spider, that crawls websites, determines the website's probable owner, and then cross-references data from the site with national databases and tax records to help find tax evaders. The Canadian tax authorities aren't the only ones using the spider.

An article in *Wired* magazine announced in January 2007:

> Websites around the world are getting a new computerized visitor among the Googlebots and Yahoo web spiders: The Taxman. A five-nation tax enforcement cartel has been quietly cracking down on suspected Internet tax cheats, using a sophisticated web crawling program to monitor transactions on auction sites, and track operators of online shops, poker and porn sites.

Named "Xenon," in reference to the auto headlights that light up dark places, this CyberSpyder program started in the Netherlands in 2004 and has been expanded with the assistance of Amsterdam-based data mining firm Sentient Machine Research. Canada is one of the five nations participating in the tax enforcement cartel, along with Austria, Denmark, the Netherlands, and the UK. Sweden is set to join this year. The CRA confirmed participation in this online tax crackdown in the *Toronto Star* in January 2007, stating that it needed "more sophisticated tools for the new age of commerce" and "there's no difference between a business on the Internet, and a business down the street. They're [both] businesses and they all have to pay their taxes."

If you are earning income from a Web-based business and aren't reporting it on your tax return, it's only a matter of time before the Agency turns its cyber eyes on you. Craigslist, EBay, and other online swap meets are not exempt from cyberscrutiny. In fact in September 2007, the Agency won a federal court order requiring EBay to turn over the names of people who are high-volume sellers on the website. But the Agency won't target you unless your transaction behaviour online is regular enough to qualify as "a business." Do be warned, though: large-dollar transactions will always attract attention. So will vehicle sales, which are always subject to government registration and payment of provincial retail sales tax. And, if you try to sell software or copyrighted music/video material without the proper licences, or guns or drugs, you can be prosecuted criminally. The RCMP has been known to show up at someone's door as a result of a suspicious online sale.

 In September 2007, the Agency won a federal court order requiring EBay to turn over the names of people who are high-volume sellers on the website.

TRACKING LESSONS FROM THE IRS

Americans already have a healthy fear of the IRS. This is because our Agency's American counterpart has already implemented measures to combat escalating tax evasion. Some of the following innovative methods could one day to come to Canada. Consider this your advance warning.

The John Doe Summons

These summonses are issued against VISA, MasterCard, American Express, and others. Using this procedure, the IRS can force the credit card issuers, under pain of continuous fines and possible prosecution, to give the names of owners of offshore credit/debit cards. This is part of an investigation to see who is using their cards to access untaxed offshore income. IRS sources indicate that the results are encouraging so far, and a large number of prosecutions against tax evaders have been, and are being, launched.

Informant Reward Programs

The IRS uses a reward program to encourage informers to come forward with credible information about their tax-evading colleagues and employers. As a reward, the informers are paid from 1% to 15% of the delinquent tax collected, up to a maximum of $2 million. Names of individuals giving the information are kept confidential and will not be disclosed. This program is so successful that the percentage of reward payable is being increased.

AN INFORMANT'S JUST REWARD?

A Colorado disc jockey received an IRS informant reward of $7,138.20 in 1998. However, he forgot one small detail. Tax is payable on the reward, and failing to report receipt of such funds is a surefire way to get the attention of the IRS. The disc jockey tax informer suddenly became a tax evader when he didn't report the reward on his return. He argued that he had shared the reward with several co-workers. In tax court, however, the judge said the letter that accompanied the reward cheque from the IRS was addressed solely to him and didn't indicate that he had an obligation to share it with anyone else. As a result, the disc jockey was ordered to pay the tax.

So far in Canada, we have drawn the line at paying such a reward. But the CRA "snitch line" is always open for inbound callers. A poll commissioned by the Agency revealed that a majority of Canadians would not turn in a friend or neighbour who was cheating on their taxes unless they were guaranteed anonymity and a great deal of money was involved in the cheating. By Canadian standards, payment for information does not seem to be very sporting. But Canadians do make extensive use of the snitch line.

Interjurisdictional Cooperation

The American trend of state and federal officials working very closely together is being emulated in Canada. This has not always been the case. In the past, Revenue Quebec, for example, did not cooperate well with its federal counterpart. That, some said, was due to its nationalist pride. But now the province of Quebec is strapped financially. Money trumps pride, and close cooperation is becoming the norm between Quebec and the federal tax authorities. A better exchange of information between the federal government and its provincial counterparts has become the order of the day.

Tracking Offshore Money

Regardless of where they live, US citizens must pay tax, after allowable deductions, on their worldwide income. Unlike Canadians, who are taxed based on residency, or on where their income is earned, Americans are taxed on the basis of citizenship. Some Americans who reside abroad have been keeping what they think are secret offshore bank and investment accounts. To their surprise, the Secretary of the Treasury and the US Attorney General are using the provisions of the Patriot Act to subpoena information from any foreign bank that does business in the United States through a correspondent bank.

Failure to comply with information requests can result in fines of US$10,000 per day and a requirement to terminate the correspondent relationship. Even SWIFT (Society for Worldwide Interbank Financial Telecommunications), which tracks the global movement of money, regularly receives compulsory subpoenas from the US government and provides it with information. Why is this important to Canada? The

IRS feeds information on Canadians to the CRA's International Tax group in Ottawa. The CRA, in turn, uses this knowledge to go after Canadian offshore tax cheats.

WHERE DOES IT ALL END?

In an age of stricter enforcement, with a tax agency possessed of policelike powers and the technology to review virtually any financial transaction in your life, the clock is ticking for all taxpayers, in particular for tax evaders. Increasingly, even honest taxpayers will find themselves treated as potential cheats. The actual cheaters are left with two choices. Wait for the CRA to find them, and suffer the consequences in court. Or come forward under a negotiated amnesty settlement. Either way, you're going to need a good tax lawyer. We recommend the amnesty route. Chapter 9 on amnesty details why.

4

TAX EVASION: PASSIVE CRIME OR ACTIVE REVOLT?

 CREDO OF THE TAX EVADER
Avoid falsehood, except for your own taxes,
which don't count because here you are not
taking somebody else's property, only trying to
safeguard your own.

What makes Canadians run the risk of incurring the Agency's wrath?

Many people feel that failure to file or disclose all their income is just being negligent—a social misdemeanour that can be cleared up with a simple apology and payment of whatever tax is owed. "I'll just pay when they catch me. . . . If they catch me!" is the most common response.

Surprise! On April Fool's Day, 2006, the Voluntary Disclosures Program (VDP) for tax delinquents who come forward on their own before being caught was moved to the Agency's Compliance Program division. The "forgiveness" or amnesty program had formerly been part of the Appeals division, which had achieved commendable success within the Agency by boosting its division's bottom line through the influx of recovered delinquent tax dollars. Jealous of Appeals' financial success,

Compliance Program lobbied to take over the amnesty program on the grounds that its more aggressive tactics would be less lenient toward tax evaders, ultimately wresting more income from them. The Agency bowed to this internal peer pressure, and Compliance Program now has jurisdiction over the VDP.

THE "TAX POLICE"

The Criminal Investigations unit of the CRA operates as part of the Taxpayer Compliance Program. Thus, Criminal Investigations has easy access to files of taxpayers who come forward to clean up past delinquencies. The possibility of criminal prosecution is more likely than ever, even when a tax evader comes forward voluntarily. Hence this warning: All taxpayers must understand that filing taxes and reporting all income accurately is not an accounting exercise, nor the fulfillment of a social obligation. It's the law.

Failure to file every year, or misrepresenting your income on your return, is tax evasion, and tax evaders are prosecuted in criminal court by way of summary conviction or upon indictment. When convicted, large fines (up to 200% of the tax that should have been paid plus daily interest) are payable. If several years have passed, the daily interest can be almost as high as the tax. There will also be civil fines of up to 50% of the tax that is owed, plus, once again, daily interest. The total can be enough to ruin you financially.

Contrary to popular opinion, declaring bankruptcy won't necessarily wipe out your tax debt. It also won't protect you from criminal charges. If you are convicted of tax evasion, you will be sent to jail if you are unable to pay the criminal penalty.

Declaring bankruptcy won't necessarily wipe out your tax debt.

"But I'm Not a Criminal . . ."

A run-in with Criminal Investigation agents from the Agency's Enforcement division (who, on the street, are called the "tax police") can lead to personal and financial ruin. Most people react by saying, "I'm not a criminal. Why am I in criminal court and being humiliated in the newspapers, and on radio and TV?"

The short answer is if you have committed criminal tax evasion, you may be tried in criminal court and, if convicted, you are a criminal.

During our combined years of tax-law practice (Paul DioGuardi has been a tax lawyer for 42 years, and Philippe DioGuardi has practised for 20 years), we have defended numerous cases where the accused faced charges of criminal tax evasion. When the CRA charges you with criminal tax evasion you are not tried in a civilized tax office, but in the same courtroom where judges preside over cases of violent crime, theft, drug trafficking, murder, and more.

It gets worse. You will be fingerprinted and have a mug shot taken. After you've been convicted, you'll also be sentenced in criminal court and have a criminal record. If you want to take a trip outside Canada, there may be difficulty crossing the border. The media is called in to report on your trial and conviction because it is government policy that everyone must know that tax cheats get caught and are punished. And, at the end of it all, your name and the details of your case will be published by the CRA and posted in the media room of its website for all the world to see. If it's a slow news day, you may find yourself headlining the local papers.

Your 15 minutes of fame could look like this:

Vancouver Resident Fined for Failing to File Tax Return

VANCOUVER, BRITISH COLUMBIA, APRIL 4, 2007. . . . Vancouver resident Jim Doe, Director of Company X, pleaded guilty yesterday in Robson Square Provincial Court to failing to comply with a notice to file the 2004 corporate income tax return. He was fined $1,000 and given 14 days to pay the fine. The outstanding return has now been filed. When people are convicted of failing to file tax returns, in addition to any fines imposed by the courts, they must still file the returns and pay the full amount of taxes owing, plus interest, as well as any civil penalties that may be assessed by the Canada Revenue Agency (CRA). Between January 2006 [sic] December 2006, compliance officers at the Burnaby-Fraser Tax Services Office obtained 16,968 late-filed tax returns. The additional taxes, penalty, and interest from those returns totalled $75,797,496.

Or this:

Compliance Program Helps to Uncover Tax Evasion by London Contractor

LONDON, ONTARIO, APRIL 24, 2007. . . . Mike Smith of London, Ontario, pleaded guilty to tax evasion in the Ontario Court of Justice in London today. He was fined $15,014, which represents 100% of the federal tax he attempted to evade.

Mr. Smith, a 52-year-old self-employed insulation installer, failed to include income of $112,465, received from a local area contractor, on his 2001 to 2004 personal income tax returns. A Canada Revenue Agency (CRA) investigation revealed that for each of the years under review, Mr. Smith failed to provide information to his tax preparer relating to the income earned from his insulation installation services. Mr. Smith indicated to the tax preparer that his sole source of income during those years was from social assistance. By not reporting this income, he attempted to evade $15,014 in federal taxes. This investigation was undertaken as a result of a program that was developed by the CRA, in consultation with the construction industry, to encourage tax compliance within the construction industry. When individuals or corporations are convicted of tax evasion, they have to pay the full amount of taxes owing, plus interest, and any penalties the CRA assesses. In addition, the court may, on summary conviction, fine them up to 200% of the taxes evaded and sentence them to a two-year jail term. Under the Income Tax Act, the CRA may also assess a penalty of up to 50% of the taxes evaded or the benefit improperly claimed.

Or, even more spectacularly, this newspaper story that appeared in the *Toronto Star* the day after the annual tax filing deadline:

Couple Jailed in Tax Evasion Case; Judge Says [Couple] Showed No Remorse

Yesterday, when most Canadians were rushing to meet the tax filing deadline, a Brampton couple landed in jail for evading taxes.

John and Jane X, who own XY Inc., got more than one shock when a judge slapped them with fines totalling almost $255,000 and 45-day terms behind bars.

The couple must pay the fines within six months. They will also have to pay the original taxes on their income over five years plus interest.

Police led the couple away in handcuffs from a Brampton court after the judge told them that they showed no remorse for dodging federal taxes both on their personal income and on the small company that they own. . . . Evidence at the trial . . . revealed that the agency conducted a net-worth assessment . . . showing the couple had assets of more than $2 million including a house, three rental properties, and a Muskoka cottage.

But [their] income in annual returns could not support their lifestyle, according to the agency. In his judgment, [the judge] also said many expense claims by the [couple] were blatant examples of the use of company funds for personal spending.

Note: We have changed the names of the individuals in all of the foregoing releases to protect their identities. The Agency was not so kind.

IS IT TIME TO WORRY?

You should be concerned about the possibility of a criminal investigation if:

- You lied on your return and now the CRA has notified you that they are reviewing it. Auditors are trained to refer cases to Investigations when they discover false or fraudulent information.
- You haven't been filing returns. If you haven't been filing, you need to be very worried. This holds true even if you think that you have paid most or all of your taxes. Wilful failure to file your tax return for more than one year if tax is due is a criminal offence.
- A third-party demand is served on your accountant, bank, employer, or others seeking information related to your taxes.
- You have problems with provincial tax authorities.

The Agency and provincial tax authorities have information-sharing agreements. Therefore, if you have a run-in with provincial tax authorities, the federal Agency may also be aware of the situation and could decide to look into the matter further.

Any of these situations indicate that the CRA is already on your case. Appropriate legal counsel is your best protection.

5

ORDINARY PEOPLE, EVERYDAY TAX TRAPS

LETTER TO AN ENGLISH TAX COLLECTOR

I wish your notices were not so agitating and did
not hold out such dreadful threats. A penalty of fifty
pounds sounds like a relic of mediaeval torture.

—*Your obedient servant,*
Oscar Wilde

Not everyone sets out to deliberately mislead the CRA. Even taxpayers who believe they are reporting their income correctly can find themselves caught in hidden tax traps. The CRA loves to go hunting and fishing, and is always sending agents into the field to fish for more tax dollars and hunt down small-time cheaters. Salaried workers, construction trades, freelancers, pensioners—you're all on the Agency's hit list. Here are some of the CRA's favourite tax traps that relate particularly, but not exclusively, to the self-employed, with some guidelines to help you avoid tripping the taxman's trap.

GST/HST COLLECTION

GST registration and collection does not apply only to corporations and registered companies. Any individual earning gross sales of $30,000 a year, or more, is required to register for, and collect and remit, GST on all sales and services.

If you work for yourself, or have a "hobby" business on the side, the federal Goods and Services Tax (GST) [or Harmonized Sales Tax (HST) if you live in New Brunswick, Nova Scotia, or Newfoundland and Labrador] can become your worst nightmare. The GST is a multistage consumption tax that became effective January 1, 1991. It is levied on the sale of most goods (products) and services sold in Canada. Only basic groceries (food), residential rents, and most health and educational services are exempt from the tax.

The seller of the goods or the provider of the service is by law compelled to register for this tax, collect it on every transaction, and then remit it to the CRA quarterly or annually. (A business or individual with sales revenues of less than $30,000 a year is not required to collect and remit GST.) Failure to collect the GST will result in the CRA assessing how much you should have collected, based on your gross sales, and then demanding payment of that sum, with penalties and interest. If you collect the GST but don't remit it on time, you are in serious trouble. Here's why:

GST is "trust money." It belongs to the government from the moment you charge it (or should have charged it). The GST legislation effectively turns you into an unpaid tax collector on behalf of the government, and you are bound to hand over the tax you collect on time. If you use the money to run your business, or to pay yourself more income, you are stealing government funds.

In Nova Scotia, New Brunswick, and Newfoundland and Labrador, a single Harmonized Sales Tax (HST) has replaced the GST and the provincial sales tax. All the pitfalls that apply to the GST apply in the same way to the HST.

GST is "trust money." If you use the money to run your business, or to pay yourself more income, you are stealing government funds.

How the Agency Can Trap You

GST infractions are the easiest of tax *faux pas* to establish because there is no grey area to debate. You must collect the tax and you must remit it to the CRA. If you don't, you can be charged criminally for tax evasion. The Agency starts out by reviewing every tax return—salaried or self-employed—to see if there is unsalaried income of any kind. And there easily can be. Perhaps you knit baby booties and sell them at craft shows. Or you sell your paintings at the local art show. Or you build decks on the weekend. Or repair boat motors. Or customize car interiors. Many people have hobby businesses on the side. The Agency will be looking at two things: Did you even report this second income on your return? And did you collect and remit the GST (or the HST, if applicable)? If your hobby income is less than $30,000, you aren't obliged to collect the GST. But the CRA will want to know why the revenue from your self-published bridge club cookbook didn't appear on your tax return. So the quest for GST can turn up more tax dollars and land you in hot water, even if it turns out GST doesn't apply to you.

FREELANCERS AS INDEPENDENT CONTRACTORS—RISK VERSUS REWARD

The costs and liabilities of being an employer can make it unaffordable for a small business to remain viable. As a result, many small companies try to convert employees into self-employed independent contractors. Employees may be happy to go along because, as contractors, they can incorporate and then be subject to a lower corporate tax rate as well as deduct the costs of sales from their taxable income. This ploy can have grave tax consequences for both the contractor and the company.

Let's say a trucking company tries to make its drivers independent contractors instead of employees. If the drivers only work for the trucking company, and do not own their vehicle, and are not individually incorporated, then the chances are that the Agency would classify them as employees, and not independent contractors. The CRA would see that, from one year to the next, the company's status had changed from paying source deductions, EI premiums, and CPP on a group of employees, to instead paying invoices to a group of drivers. The red flag would go up, and the field agent would drop by the company's offices to see if the trucks going in and out were privately owned by the drivers, or part of the company's fleet. That would trigger an audit, trapping both the company owners and the drivers. The drivers' billings would be reclassified as salary and taxed, most likely, at a higher rate. The drivers would also be reassessed for all deductions claimed as costs of operating their business, with interest and penalties added in. The resulting tax bill could easily be enough to destroy the drivers financially. The company owner similarly could be driven to the point of ruin. All money paid out to the various drivers would be reclassified as salary, and subject to employer source deductions, plus employer contributions for CPP and EI, with interest and penalties.

Other areas where this strategy is frequent—and dangerous—include cleaning companies, limousine services, spas and hair salons, film production companies and post-production studios, and more.

INDEPENDENT CONTRACTOR OR EMPLOYEE? A LITMUS TEST.

- Do you mostly/always work out of your client's premises? *Yes/No*
- Does your client provide:
  Your computer? *Yes/No*
  Cellphone? *Yes/No*
  Vehicle/transportation? *Yes/No*
  Equipment/tools *Yes/No*
- Is more than 90% of your business income from one client? *Yes/No*
- Does your client provide you with medical, dental, or insurance benefits? *Yes/No*
- Do you bill your client as an individual (as opposed to through an incorporated company)? *Yes/No*

If you answered *Yes* to all or most of these questions, the CRA could interpret your working relationship as being that of an employee.

How to Protect Your Status as an Independent Contractor

Incorporate your business. This legitimizes your intent to operate your own business independently of the companies you work for. Be advised, though, that a corporation is a separate legal entity, with its own set of obligations for tax filing and tax payments in addition to what you will be required to file and pay as an individual who receives income from your corporation. Your corporation may be required to register for and remit GST, depending upon the nature of your business and its annual revenue. You may also be required to collect and remit provincial retail sales tax.

Maintain your own business premises. The nature of your work—freelance copywriter, perhaps, or independent tutor—may demand that you provide your services at your client's place of work. However, your business should have a head office that is not within your client's premises. You don't have to run out and rent a space. You may designate a specific area of your home and claim deductions for a portion of the cost of rent/mortgage, heat, and even furniture acquisitions relative to the percentage of the home legitimately devoted to your business.

Provide your own equipment. You should own your computer, your telephone, your cellphone, and any equipment or tools unique to your trade (brushes, scissors, styling products, etc., if you're a hair stylist renting a chair at a salon; ladders, drills, hammers, etc., if you're a carpenter; mops, brooms, buckets, cleaning supplies, etc., if you're an office or home cleaner). You can charge your clients for costs associated with the use of this equipment and deduct your costs from your gross sales.

Have a written work-services agreement with your client. This demonstrates the intent on both your parts to maintain an independent working relationship.

Do not accept benefits offered to salaried employees. As a contractor, you are not eligible for the company pension plan or health and dental benefits. Accepting these as part of your remuneration may disqualify you as an independent contractor. It is possible to write a performance-based bonus into your contract, which is a way for you to receive extra fees based upon your contribution to the success of your client's business.

Ensure all your invoices come from the corporation, not you personally. This further establishes the legitimacy of your independent enterprise.

Keep accurate records. This way, if challenged, you can demonstrate to the CRA that you are operating a legitimate business.

File your taxes on time and pay tax owing promptly. Don't give the Agency a reason to keep looking at your tax file.

EMPLOYEE OR SELF-EMPLOYED?

Indicators That the Worker Is an Employee
- The payer directs and controls many elements of work performance (such as what, who, where, when, and how).
- The payer controls the worker's absences, such as sick leave or vacation leave.
- The payer controls the worker with respect to the results of the work and the method used to do the work.
- The payer creates the work schedule and establishes the worker's rules of conduct.
- The worker must perform the work.
- The worker must remit activity reports to the payer.
- The worker's activities are reserved to a single payer (exclusivity of services).
- The payer can impose disciplinary actions on a worker.
- The worker receives training or direction from the payer on how to perform the work.
- The worker accepts integration into the payer's business to have the latter benefit from his work.
- The parties have inserted a non-competition clause in their written contract.

Indicators That the Worker Is Self-Employed

- The worker is usually free to work when and for whom he chooses and may provide his or her services to different payers at the same time.
- The worker does not have to perform the services personally. He or she can hire another party to either complete the work or help complete the work.
- The worker can generally choose the time and the manner the work will be performed.
- The worker does not need to be at the payer's premises.
- The worker can accept or refuse work from the payer.
- The working relationship between the payer and the worker does not present a degree of continuity, loyalty, security, subordination, or integration, all of which are generally associated with an employer-employee relationship.

INCOME SPLITTING AND EMPLOYING FAMILY MEMBERS

In the spirit of arranging one's affairs to pay as little tax as is necessary, many owner-operated businesses put family members, such as spouses, children, and siblings, on the company payroll to reduce the business' taxable income. The Agency tracks this with its matching program, and it usually throws up a red flag for further investigation.

How the Agency Can Trap You

The Agency will send a field agent out to visit the business. This agent will try to talk to employees without the owner being present. The agent will casually ask, "Does Mrs. Smith [the owner's wife] work here, too? Is she in the office every day? What does she do here? Does she ever take money out of the cash register?" Caught off guard, a chatty employee will often reveal that Mrs. Smith is in only once or twice a week—if that—and, when she does come in, she usually sits in the owner's office and makes personal phone calls. Or perhaps she does answer the phones, or manages the bookkeeping. The field agent will cross-reference this information against what Mrs. Smith is paid. Is it in keeping with what a receptionist or bookkeeper is usually paid? If Mrs. Smith is being paid $80,000 a year for these duties, the CRA will want to look more closely into what is really going on. This is especially true if the money paid to her is not salaried income, but simply a transaction on the books. Then the CRA will review whether or not she is paid regularly and at the same intervals as the other staff. The CRA's goal is to establish that these payments are a) not reasonable for the service supposedly provided, and b) not an arm's-length transaction between an owner and a contractor.

How You Can Protect Yourself

- Ensure that family members provide legitimate services at a reasonable market value.
- If you are not paying the family member on salary, ensure that he or she issues you regular invoices for the services provided.
- Pay the family member as you would any other contractor, by cheque, and in a timely manner.
- Don't forget to factor in the cost of GST if the family member is billing more than $30,000 a year.
- Consult with your accountant or other tax-planning professional about the appropriate structure for your business.
- Consider incorporating. Your family members can become shareholders of the corporation, which allows you to pay them dividends, whether they actually perform services or not.

Dividends are typically taxed at a lower rate than employment income, which may help you better achieve your end objective, which is to arrange your affairs legitimately to pay less tax.

BUILDING-TRADE CONTRACTORS

Across Canada, and especially in large cities, the home-renovation business is booming. Small, independent contractors—carpenters, plumbers, drywallers, builders—often carry out the work. They are sometimes quite happy to offer homeowners an attractive discount in return for cash under the table. These tradespeople often play a canny shell game with the Agency, filing tax returns that show a "reasonable" income but not disclosing the full sum of their sales. There are dangers for both the contractor and all the subtrades who work for him or her. If the contractor is caught, the Agency will automatically review all the subcontractors working for him or her. If a subcontractor is caught, the Agency will review the contractor. The homeowner who knowingly participates can also face consequences.

How the Agency Traps Contractors and Subcontractors

Tax cheating is notoriously rampant in the home-renovation business, which means the Agency is systemically monitoring all players in the industry, including the honest tax filers. One of the Agency's favourite ways to spot the cheaters is by accessing the contractor discount program files at Rona, The Home Depot, and the other large supplier retailers. These discount programs log all the purchases made by an individual contractor or business. It's very easy for the Agency to cross-reference the purchase records with the contractor's reported business income. If the numbers don't add up, the red flag goes up.

The CRA also uses other sources to track tax fraud, including the Contract Payment Reporting System (CPRS), Workers' Compensation Board reports, business and lifestyle audits, and complaints by home-owners, angry neighbours, and the like.

BUILDING-TRADE PERILS

Over the last two years (tax years 2005 and 2006), the Agency's enforcement actions in the construction sector have resulted in:

- 24,944 audits
- $140 million in federal taxes assessed
- $44 million dollars in interest and penalties
- $36 million in disqualified GST/HST New Housing Rebates
- $88 million unreported income detected through the Contract Payment Reporting System (CPRS)
- 58,903 non-filer and non-registrant (GST/HST) tax returns

The consequences of tax evasion apply to all those contractors, and their subcontractors, who are caught. Penalties and interest, in addition to the tax assessed owing for all the years in question, can add up to a staggering amount. Contractors may also be prosecuted criminally, resulting in further fines and interest, and may find their professional reputations destroyed when their names and the details of their convictions are published by the CRA. In some cases, particularly in a repeat situation, where tax evasion on a large scale is involved, the courts may also impose a jail sentence.

Consequences for the Homeowner

As the party who has engaged the contractor for cash, it would be difficult for the CRA to hold the homeowner responsible for unfiled tax returns or dishonest income reporting. However, agreeing to pay cash for a project may expose the homeowner to collection of GST monies. It may be possible for the CRA to recover the GST that should have been collected by the contractor on the gross total of the "sale" from the homeowner who should have paid it.

It is in your best interest as a homeowner to specify, even in a cash sale, that you expect the agreed price to include the GST. Put it in writing and get the contractor to sign it. If he refuses, you'll have a pretty good indication that he is not fulfilling his tax obligations, and if you proceed, you do so at your own peril.

How Builders and Tradespeople Can Protect Themselves

- Create a written contract with the homeowner for each project, even if payment is received in cash.
- Ensure that all prices quoted include GST.
- Draw up a proper payment contract for all subcontractors.
- Report all income accurately on your tax return.
- File every year.
- Report all cash payments received.
- Ensure GST is collected and remitted as required.
- Don't be persuaded to drop your price to take cash under the table. A homeowner who insists on this form of payment is looking for a bargain at your expense.

RESTAURANT WAITSTAFF, ESTHETICIANS, BELLHOPS, AND SIMILAR WORKERS

If you're a server in a restaurant or bar, or an esthetician in a spa, or a bellhop at a big hotel, or if you work in any other service role where people often give you a cash gratuity, your tips aren't considered a lucky windfall. You have to report them in addition to your salary—even if you don't have receipts.

The Tip Project: The Agency's Favourite Field Trip (and Tax Trap)

Workers in service jobs are under constant scrutiny. The Agency maintains lists of hotels, restaurants, spas, and hair salons. Through the matching program it can target all the employees of a specific bar, hotel, or spa, and compare salaries and "other income reported." One overly honest waitress or bellhop can condemn the rest of staff to a reassessment or audit. Even worse, the Agency may send agents into the field on what they call a "Tip Project." The agent will pose as a customer and visit the hotel, restaurant, or bar on the busiest day of the week at the busiest time. The agent will observe how much the server or bellhop appears to receive in tips. (In some cases, the agent will even offer the server an exceptionally large tip.) The agent will then use the tips earned during that "peak period" as the benchmark for the tips earned on a consistent basis, and issue an income reassessment based on that amount for all the servers or bellhops in the restaurant or hotel. It's up to the servers and bellhops to prove the assessment is wrong. Not easy when a field agent has first-hand evidence.

Even more insidious, the Agency may single out one of the servers or bellhops for reassessment and then offer to waive penalties, interest, and prosecution if that person agrees to amend his or her tax return to show the proper amount of gratuity income. The CRA will then use that evidence to reassess all the other servers or bellhops for unreported gratuities of the same amount.

At the end of the day, the field trip puts more tax dollars into the Agency's coffers. One can also imagine that a visit to a hotel bar or fine restaurant is a pleasant enough assignment.

How You Can Protect Yourself

- Keep a daily record of the tips you receive. Jot them down in a pocket notebook.
- Report all gratuities accurately on your tax return.
- Share your "process" with your co-workers and suggest they do the same.
- Retain all your records so you can refute an inflated reassessment.
- Immediately contact a tax lawyer if you are approached by the CRA to "cut a deal" as described above. You have the right to retain counsel to protect yourself against self-incrimination, regardless of what the Agency may say. For instance, the Agency may suggest that it would be better to handle this one-to-one, or even threaten more serious consequences if you retain a lawyer. Remember the advice in Chapter 1: don't trust the Agency to honour a verbal agreement.

TAXI DRIVERS AND OWNERS

The Agency uses a different sting to extract more tax from taxi drivers. The matching program makes it easy to review the income reported from all the drivers who own and operate cabs for a specific cab company. The anomalies can direct the Agency to the under-reporting drivers—typically those who report enough income to cover the costs of their "stand rent" and not much more. Then the sting swings into action.

The Taxi Project: Another Favourite Tax Trap

The Agency contacts one of the taxi owners and suggests that he or she is losing out on important government benefits by not reporting all of his or her income. For instance, by reporting at least $15,000 in annual income, the driver can qualify to pay into the Canada Pension Plan and receive a retirement benefit. If the driver agrees to sign a declaration saying that he or she has unreported income and is prepared to file an amended tax return, the CRA can agree to waive the penalties and interest as well as not prosecute for criminal tax evasion. As soon as the amended return is filed, the Agency uses that information to reassess all the other drivers in the company at a similar income level, capturing more tax dollars through the additional tax, plus interest and penalties.

How You Can Protect Yourself

- Report all your income accurately.
- Consult with an accredited tax professional about benefits that you may be entitled to, including CPP.
- Follow the same counsel we offered to service staff: immediately contact a tax lawyer if you are approached by the CRA to "cut a deal—" and for all the same reasons.

CHILDCARE PROVIDERS, BABYSITTERS, CLEANERS, HOUSEKEEPERS, AND OTHER IN-HOME HELP

Many people choose to work independently as nannies, babysitters, housekeepers, house cleaners, or in-home care providers. This means you go to your client's home to work, and you have a direct working relationship with the people who pay you, usually the baby's or child's parents, the homeowner, or the person who receives your care. These working relationships are often conducted on a cash basis. But the Agency still expects its share—or at least demands that you report all the cash you earn on your tax returns.

How the Agency Can Trap You

A number of things can trigger the Agency's red flag. Perhaps a couple is applying for a loan or mortgage and, to make their income look better, they include the income from the wife's work as a childcare provider. Or the parents of a child may claim a deduction for the money they pay for childcare services. Perhaps you provide cleaning services to someone who works from home. Your client will likely claim the cost of your services as a business expense. In either case, the parents or the business owner need to be prepared to provide the name and details of the person to whom fees were paid. Suddenly the CRA has a trail that leads straight to you—the babysitter or the cleaning lady.

There's more at stake than simply reporting your income and paying tax on it. Just as important is the determination of whether you are working as an employee or as a self-employed service provider. If you are considered self-employed, then you are solely responsible for reporting your income and paying tax on it. If you are considered an employee, then your client will face substantial tax and reporting responsibilities on your behalf.

According to the CRA's guidelines, the amount of control your client (the parent or homeowner, etc.) has over your work determines whether or not you are self-employed. If you control the number of hours you work, where you work, which materials you use, and the way in which you perform your duties, you will most likely be considered self-employed. If you work at the employer's home and the employer specifies the work to be done, the working hours, and supervises your work, you will most likely be considered an employee.

It's in the CRA's best interest to have you classified as an employee, since you will be required to contribute to CPP and EI, and you will not be able to deduct certain costs from your income, including the expense of travel to and from your workplace. This determination also has serious and costly consequences for the person who hires you. As an employer, your client will be obliged to deduct payroll taxes at source, deduct contributions for EI and CPP, and make the requisite employer contributions on your behalf to these programs. Overtime may also be mandatory, depending on the service you provide and the hours you work. Your employer will also be expected to provide you with a T4 form each year for the purposes of your own tax filing. An employer is also obliged to keep accurate records and remit all source deductions and employer contributions in full and on time. If the nanny or housekeeper is, in fact, an employee, this can add thousands of dollars a year to the employer's costs, not to say anything of the record-keeping and remittance responsibilities.

Get it wrong, and the Agency will be after your employer and you, the employee.

THIS REALLY HAPPENED TO AN UNSUSPECTING WORKING MOTHER

Jan Trent was a working mother with a toddler at home. She hired a babysitter to come to her home five days a week to look after the child. The nanny was paid by cheque every week and provided Jan with receipts, which she used to claim a deduction for childcare expenses each year.

After a couple of years, Jan had a second child and decided to stay home for a time. One day, about six months after the nanny had stopped working for her, there was a knock at her door. A man in a dark suit with a briefcase was standing on her porch.

"Mrs. Trent?" he said. "I'm John Talent from the Canada

Revenue Agency, and I would like to review the books for your business."

Jan was dumbfounded. "I don't run a business," she said.

"Our records show that you employed a certain [nanny] for a period of two and half years between [dates]. Is this correct?"

Jan agreed that this was so. "But she was simply a babysitter who looked after my son."

The CRA agent proceeded to fire off a list of questions: Did the babysitter come to your home five days a week or more? Yes. Did you determine what time she arrived and left? Yes. Did you determine the duties she was to perform? Yes. Did you allow her time off for sickness and vacation? Yes. The questions went on and on. At the end, Agent Talent, while sympathetic to Jan's situation, quietly said, "We have determined that during the time [the nanny] worked for you, she was an employee, and we will therefore be reassessing you for source deductions and employer contributions relative to that period."

Sure enough, a few weeks later Jan received an assessment for several thousand dollars, including penalties and interest, which she had no choice but to pay. "Who knew?" Jan said when she recounted the story to family and friends.

Jan didn't know, but now you do.

How You Can Protect Yourself

If You're Doing the Hiring

• Draw up a written contract if you intend to hire a babysitter (or any in-home helper) as a self-employed service provider, and specify that you do not have an employer/employee relationship and that the service provider will be responsible for all tax liabilities.

- Review the contract with a qualified tax professional to ensure it protects you.
- Insist on a receipt every time you pay the service provider, even if payment is made in cash.
- Maintain accurate reports of the money paid to your service provider so that you can respond to any questions about deductions on your tax return.
- If a tax agent arrives at your door and does not produce a search warrant, politely decline to speak with him or her until you have discussed the situation with appropriate legal counsel.
- Do not allow yourself to be intimidated by the tax agent, and do not respond to any questions without the protection of your legal counsel.

If You're Being Hired
- Discuss upfront with your client that you are working as a self-employed service provider and that you are not interested in an employee/employer relationship.
- Protect your intent by providing your client with a written contract stating the duties that you will perform, the days and times you will be available to perform them, when you require payment for your services, and how much you are to be paid.
- Remember that, as a self-employed service provider, you are required to maintain accurate records of your sources of income and report them accurately on your tax return every year. To that end, you should issue an invoice to your client for the payments due to you. You may choose to receive payment in cash or by cheque, but all payment received must be recorded accurately.
- If your gross annual income from your self-employed work exceeds $30,000, you are required to register for GST, and must collect and remit that amount as required by the tax authorities.

You must add that cost to your invoices and insist that your client pays it to you in addition to your fees for service.

- Review your situation with a qualified tax professional to determine if you should continue to work as a self-employed individual, or whether there would be tax-saving advantages or other benefits if you became a business or a corporation.
- Do not be intimidated by an aggressive would-be client who refuses to sign your work contract. Inform the client that this relationship is also in his or her best interest. (You can share Jan's story, above.) If the client still refuses, keep looking for another position. In today's working environment, qualified nannies and impeccable housekeepers are worth their weight in gold and you can afford to insist on a proper working relationship.
- Above all, understand that working for cash under the table is illegal and, if you choose to operate in this manner, you will always be at risk of discovery.
- If you receive any communication from the CRA demanding filing of tax returns, or questioning the nature of your working relationship with your employer, do not respond until you have consulted appropriate legal tax counsel.

THE CASE OF THE NON-FILING CONSULTANT

About five years ago, my business went through a tough patch. I'd been working out of town on contract, and then ran into some personal problems that made it difficult for me to work. So I wrapped up that project and moved back home, and I tried to get things going again. It cost me a lot of money to change cities. And then I had trouble lining up new clients right away, and I wasn't well. It just all got away from me.

When it came time for corporate year end, I didn't have it in me to go through all the bookkeeping and do a tax return. I didn't have any money in the bank to pay a tax bill, anyway. So, one way or another, the deadline slipped by. And I still wasn't really working. I thought I'd get it all fixed up before the next year. I wasn't all that stressed about it. It was just a tax return. I'd been paying taxes—huge amounts of taxes—every year without fail for all the years I'd been working. Almost for 20 years, I guess. And this one year I run into a tough patch and—BAM!—the taxman's on my case like a ton of bricks.

Out of the blue, I started getting these letters. And phone calls. It started with a Demand to File, or something. I wasn't in a very good mindset at the time. I'd go for weeks at a time without opening my mail. So I can't honestly say that I really knew there was a problem. But it took a couple of years before things started to get ugly. That's when I found myself facing this really ugly summons to attend court to face criminal charges.

It was bizarre. I'm being hauled up in criminal court because I didn't send in my taxes. Anyway, when I got this summons I called a lawyer friend and for minute he didn't say anything. Then his voice turned really serious, and he told me that this was for real. He said I had to go down to the courthouse for the arraignment, and that I'd need to retain legal counsel.

I was blown away. I wasn't thinking of it as tax evasion. I just didn't send in my taxes. I just thought it was an accounting thing. The idea that it was a criminal offence never crossed my mind.

I had to go into court and stand there, in the courtroom, next to the punks who were in for various adventures from the night before. There I am, in my grey suit, looking at the judge as he set a date for my trial and sent me away. It was like being on another planet.

The actual trial was just as bad. The judge sat up there on the bench. And the two lawyers—the one from the Crown and my defence lawyer—they're flapping around the courtroom in black robes looking like crows, or something. The Crown demanded all my past years of tax records from my accounting firm. One of the accountants was even called in as a witness against me. They had bank statements and credit card records. It was everything about every penny I'd ever had. And then, at the end, I had to stand there and listen to the judge tell me that I had been found guilty on two counts of tax evasion. One for not filing personal tax returns, and one for failing to file and remit my GST.

It's not like there was even a lot of money owed. The total income that they were saying I didn't report each year wasn't even six figures. You'd think the tax people should be spending their time chasing down the million-dollar corporations, instead of harassing a guy like me.

I still don't believe this happened to me. I didn't hurt anybody. In fact, the only person who got hurt was me. I guess I just didn't know it could get that serious.

The bottom line: the CRA will not magically go away just because business is bad.

6

TRAPPING THE T4S—WHEN DEDUCTIONS AT SOURCE AREN'T ENOUGH

Dear Canada Revenue Agency,
Please remove my name from your mailing list. . .

Salaried workers have their income tax, CPP, and EI premiums deducted at source and remitted to the CRA by their employer. It's money they never see. How, then, can the Agency set traps for them?

You'd be surprised. Even the most punctilious, T4'd, salaried employee can find the Agency at his door. This chapter discusses some of the more obvious ways ordinary, honest folks trip up.

RESIDENTIAL RENTAL INCOME

With residential real estate prices sky high in major cities across the country, many homeowners count on renting out an apartment in the basement or up on the third floor to help cover the cost of their mortgage and the property taxes. Any rent you charge must be declared in full as a part of your taxable income. You can offset this income by deducting certain costs, including maintenance and improvements. But many people choose to forgo the deductions by simply not reporting the income.

How the Agency Can Trap You

Remember the Agency's matching program? One of the things it scans for are the rental addresses of students who are able to claim a deduction for accommodation while away at college or university. Here's how a scenario can play out: You rent your basement apartment to a nice, young graduate student, who asks you for rent receipts. You know she's spending all her resources on tuition, so you're happy to help her net a small tax refund. But when she files her tax return, the matching program shows that you, the owner of the address she has listed, have only reported your T4-salaried income. The discrepancy buzzer goes off, and an agent is dispatched into the field to knock on your door and ask if you have an apartment for rent. The agent looks like yet another older student looking for accommodation, and you regretfully say no, your only space is already rented. Gotcha! Expect a reassessment notice—going back for as many years as the CRA can establish you have had an apartment to rent. Maybe it was a nosy neighbour who phoned the Agency snitch line on you (read more about this in Chapter 7), or you had a dispute with a former tenant who decided to get revenge.

Even your tenants can have hassles with the Agency, and their problems can lead the taxman to your door.

THE CASE OF THE SUBLEASING STUDENT

Between her second and third year at university, Linda decided to stay near campus and work for the summer. She subleased a room in a house already leased by five other students and moved in for June, July, and August. In September she moved back into a college dorm. Come tax time the following April, she visited her accountant, who—in the manner of a good accountant—inquired about where she had lived while working away from home. The accountant asked if Linda had receipts for her rent paid in June, July, and August, which Linda produced. The accountant entered a deduction for the rent paid, and the tax return was efiled. A month later, Linda received a small refund of about $150. Three months after that she received a letter from the CRA challenging her rent deduction and demanding that she produce her rental receipts along with a list of the names and social insurance numbers of the five other students who were also tenants in the house. She had 30 days in which to respond.

Linda asked her accountant for help and was advised to provide the CRA with everything they demanded. Linda approached the other students, who were reluctant to provide their personal information but eventually agreed. The accountant sent Linda's receipts and the other information back to the CRA. A month later, Linda was sent a reassessment notice. The refund she had received in June was reduced by $35, which she was required to repay, with interest, immediately. She also received a bill from her accountant for $150. Meanwhile, the five students living in the house were sent notices requiring them to establish that Linda's subrental income had been accounted for in their statement of rental expenses.

Undoubtedly, the owner of the leased house was also subjected to a review.

Landlords

- Always have a written lease agreement specifying the rent to be paid to you. This way you can prove how much income you derived from the rental.
- Report all the rental income on your tax return. Yes, it will likely increase your tax rate and may increase the income payable on your salary. But you will be able to offset any increase by deducting the costs of maintaining and upgrading the rental unit. And if you can't afford an additional tax hit on your salary, then you should forgo the rental and just pay for your housing costs all on your own. Making extra money on the side without reporting it is tax evasion and absolutely against the law.

Tenants

- Always have a written lease agreement specifying the rent you are to pay. This way you can claim any accommodation deductions that are allowed.
- If you share a lease with others, make it clear that you will be claiming a deduction, and ask your roommates to be prepared to provide you with personal information in case it is requested by the CRA.

SENIORS WITH FOREIGN PENSIONS

Many seniors don't realize that pensions paid out to them by a foreign government must be declared as part of their taxable income each year—even though that income may not be taxable if the senior was still resident in that country. (This applies particularly to recipients of

UK pensions.) As a result, seniors can accumulate 10 or 20 years of income that has never been reported. It can add up to a horrendous tax problem when it comes to light. And the Agency will not take pity on you just because you're an elderly gentleman or somebody's kindly grandmother.

How the Agency Can Trap You

Unreported foreign pension certainly will appear during an assessment or audit. Otherwise it's most likely to be revealed when your heirs settle your estate. The Agency will question the source of the income that cannot be accounted for in the senior's employee pension, Canada Pension Plan, or OAS benefits. In some cases, the senior's heirs are not even aware that there is a foreign pension. The burden to pay the tax, with civil penalties and daily interest, falls on them and must be discharged before the estate can clear probate. It's not a pleasant legacy to leave behind. Many seniors, once they realize that they have been evading tax, consider the amnesty option.

How You Can Protect Yourself

- The best protection is to report all sources of income received from anywhere in the world. Omitting any income source creates a scenario of "I didn't know I was supposed to report that." This carries absolutely no weight with the Agency.
- Ask a tax professional to assess your income and help you accurately report everything. A well-informed tax professional will know what income sources are subject to income tax.
- Most important, if you haven't been reporting your foreign pension income, seek an amnesty before you file your next return.

HOBBY OR BUSINESS?

When does your after-hours activity become a viable business? Maybe never. But if you sell what you make, paint, write, or create, or offer a service, the income must be reported on your tax return.

The rule of thumb is something like this: Hold a garage sale once and, unless you were selling cars or priceless works of art, the Agency isn't likely to demand that you declare the income. Hold a garage sale once every month, or once a week, or at some other regular interval, and two things will happen. First, you may be subject to provincial retail sales tax as a vendor, and you may also be required to collect and remit GST. Second, the CRA will reassess you for the revenue from your garage sales, which, when added to your salaried income, may also bump you into a higher tax bracket.

Here's a partial list of activities that could be deemed as revenue-generating businesses:
- dressmaking and costuming
- carpentry
- baking
- making custom cards or scrapbooks
- paintings and portraiture
- photography, particularly of weddings, pets, and families
- car servicing or custom detailing
- giving music lessons, dance lessons, drama classes
- giving performances for which you are paid
- equipment/vehicle renting
- tutoring, in your home or in the student's
- babysitting, in your home or in the child's
- dog walking and pet sitting
- gardening and/or lawn care
- life coaching
- self-publishing books, including cookbooks or journals

No matter how much or how little it is, if you receive any income from an activity, report it on your tax return.

How You Can Protect Yourself

- Review your hobby activity with a tax professional to ensure the income is reported appropriately. If you are advised to "forget about the income," get a second opinion. If it's not taxable, the Agency won't tax you on it. It's always safer to report first and get a refund later.
- Since you are reporting your income, you may also be eligible to deduct the costs of creating the materials that generated the income. If so, claim the deductions and reap the tax rewards.

SERIAL HOUSE FLIPPERS

If a home is your principal residence when you sell it, and you have lived in it for at least one year, you don't have to report any capital gain on the sale. However, if at some point during the time you owned the property it was not your principal residence, you may have to report all or part of the capital gain on your income tax return. If you work from your home, or run a business from your home and deduct capital cost allowance for renovations or additions you have made to the home in order to accommodate the business, capital gain and recapture rules will apply when you sell your home.

The Agency may start to take note of the capital gains on the sale of your residences and assess it as taxable income.

Renovations to your home can substantially enhance its value, but you will not be required to report this as a capital gain when you sell the home, provided it was your principal residence. But what happens when renovating the house you live in becomes your business, and you make your income by selling the home you have just renovated?

If the buy-renovate-sell cycle is demonstrably your principal source of income, and if you do it repeatedly, the Agency may start to take note of the capital gains on the sale of your residences and assess it as taxable income.

How the Agency Can Trap You

The first red flag that could come to the Agency's attention is the regular appearance of expense deductions on your tax return. If you are repeatedly claiming deductions for home improvements, and your principal residence address changes every couple of years, the CRA will likely put two and two together and start looking for an opportunity to assess your home sales as business income.

The Agency may check to see if you have a contractor's account at the local Home Depot or Rona store, and look into how much you spend each year buying home renovation materials. If you're continually buying the makings of a new kitchen or new bathrooms, it will show up on your account purchases.

One day, you may choose a home in a neighbourhood that is reno'd out—meaning the other people who live on the street are so tired of renovations that they've started complaining. It only takes one call to the Agency snitch line to set the CRA investigative team in motion.

Unusual circumstances can also cause you to be targeted to pay the capital gains tax. Take the case of the big-city businessman who purchased a house adjacent to the home he was renovating so that his family would have a comfortable place to live in during the renovations. Once work was finished on the first home, he put up the temporary home for sale. The Agency decided to charge him capital gains tax on the sale of the second home, despite the fact that his family had lived in that home during the year of the renovation of the first home. Why? Because both homes were in his name, and the Agency maintained that he could have only one principal residence at a time. He had designated the first home purchased as the principal residence, forcing the definition of second home on the home in which his family had lived for the year. Fortunately, the second home was resold within months of when it was purchased, and the capital gain was minimal.

How You Can Protect Yourself

- Seek professional tax advice at the outset of your buy-reno-vate-sell cycle. You should know before you start whether you will be subject to the capital gains tax.
- If your intent is to earn all or most of your income flipping houses, acknowledge that this is your business and set up a proper structure for income reporting and tax remittance.
- Be aware that the Agency will be watching for this activity and govern yourself accordingly. Penalties and interest on unreported income over several years from the sale of several houses can ruin you financially.

IF YOU ARE A SALARIED (T4'D) EMPLOYEE

Even the most conscientious, T4-salaried, always-file-on-time Canadian stands in danger of the Agency's scrutiny. Don't forget that the Agency has copies of all your T4 slips and checks to see that you have reported your income correctly. Following are some things to keep in mind when reporting your income.

Almost any benefit that your employer provides to you is considered taxable and its value should be added to your taxable income for deductions at source. This is a classic trap for T4-salaried employees. Some typical taxable benefits are:

- a vehicle provided by your employer
- fuel and mileage allowance paid to you (versus a reimbursement)
- cellphone, BlackBerry, iPhone, and airtime
- food and lodging, such as the reward trip to Hawaii, the weekend away to celebrate the sales-team victory, a company party and overnight stay at a country inn, especially when your spouse or other guest is included
- the flat-screen TV you "won" for referring new employees

How the Agency Can Trap You

A conscientious employer will automatically account for the value of any of these benefits and add it to your taxable income and make the appropriate source deductions. It will definitely hurt when you see how much you were assessed for taxation purposes without ever having seen the money in your bank account. But it will hurt less than receiving an assessment notice at tax time requesting thousands of dollars more.

Not all employers make allowance for these extras. If they don't, the onus is on you to declare the value of the benefit on your tax return. All it takes is one employee in the company to dutifully declare that he also uses the company car for personal driving, and the matching program will seek out everyone with a similar car benefit and assess you all for tax on the benefit. A company audit could also trigger a CRA investigation of employee benefits.

- Discuss the value of any benefits and the company's tax accounting practices with your employer to ensure tax on any benefits is deducted at source.
- If you are not certain about a benefit's tax status, consult a tax professional. Report the value of the benefit if so advised.
- If you drive a company vehicle, keep an accurate mileage log of all business trips and all personal trips. Remember that the commute from your home to the office is not considered business travel.
- Also keep a record of your business use of your cellphone, BlackBerry, and other mobile-communications equipment. If your company is ever audited, you may need to substantiate the percentage of your usage that was for business purposes.

A FINAL WARNING FOR THE T4'D

None of the aforementioned scenarios may apply to you. But the Agency can still trap you for one simple oversight: not filing your tax return every year.

In our tax law practice, we see more and more people who are T4'd and simply have not filed for five, six, and even more years. They have been treating it as an administrative matter and ignoring numerous requests coming from the Canada Revenue Agency to file, with little understanding that their situation is morphing into a possible criminal prosecution.

How the Agency Can Trap You

Provision 150(2) of the Income Tax Act allows the CRA to demand that a return be filed for a designated taxation year. This can be required whether or not the person in question owes any taxes. Failure to file the return after a demand was sent constitutes a criminal offence punishable on summary conviction. As a taxpayer, you cannot abdicate your duty to prepare a tax return to a third-party tax preparer and then say: "It was my accountant's fault the return was not filed." This defence usually carries little weight in court.

The importance of Provision 150(2) is that anyone, even a person who is T4'd, can be prosecuted by the CRA for failure to file.

The situation is even more serious if it turns out that, despite your at-source deductions, there is still tax owing. In that case, under Provision 162(1), failure to file an annual return carries a penalty of 5% of the year's unpaid tax, plus 1% per month (up to 12 months) from the due date. Failure to file an annual return after a Demand to File is made (subsequent occurrence within three years) carries a penalty of 10% of the unpaid tax for the year plus 2% per month (up to 20 months) from the due date.

How You Can Protect Yourself

File your tax return every year, preferably on time. And if you haven't been filing, clean up your act now. Start with a tax amnesty. Once that has been granted you can move on to filing the past-due returns.

1

THE HEAVY ARTILLERY—A TAXPAYER'S GUIDE TO THE AGENCY'S TOP 10 TACTICS AND TECHNIQUES

Knowing an opponent's tactics in advance gives you the opportunity to prepare an effective offensive strategy. Here we present an overview of the top 10 tactics and techniques the CRA employs to assess tax and enforce payment.

1. NET-WORTH ASSESSMENTS (SOMETIMES CALLED ARBITRARY OR LIFESTYLE ASSESSMENTS)

When: If a tax return isn't filed, or when the CRA is suspicious of the income declared on a filed tax return

What: A net-worth assessment takes a taxpayer's net worth (i.e., the cost of assets less liabilities) at the beginning of a year and compares it with the taxpayer's net worth at the end of a subsequent year. Expenditures for the period are added into the total. The resulting figure is assumed to be the taxpayer's income unless the taxpayer establishes the contrary. Usually, the Agency will select a period of at least three or four consecutive years for this analysis.

Stealth investigators will go into the field to personally review your lifestyle. They will sit outside your home to see who lives there, who goes in and out, how it is maintained and furnished, and what type of car, or cars, you drive. They will ask your neighbours about you. They will follow your car to see where you take your children to school, where you go to do business every day, and with whom you do business. They will monitor how often you travel, where you go, and what you declare when you return. They will demand full access to your bank account and credit card statements, which the financial institutions must by law provide. Think of it as the "tax police" turned private eye.

The Agency's Advantage: The Agency can use whatever it sees, hears, and discovers to come up with a net-worth assessment of you, which is then compared to the information disclosed on your tax return. The CRA will use any discrepancies as the foundation for a reassessment, an audit, or a criminal investigation. At the very least, a net-worth assessment generally results in a highly inflated estimate of income earned.

Danger to the Taxpayer: You may be unaware of the seriousness of your situation until, one day, you receive your reassessment, Notice of Audit, or notice that a criminal investigation is underway. At that time, the onus of proof will be entirely on you to refute the Agency's findings. (Exception: If charged with criminal tax evasion, you will then be protected by the Charter of Rights, and in a court of law the onus will be on the Agency to prove beyond a reasonable doubt the validity of the charges against you. Even so, this is not a place you ever want to be.)

Your assessment will undoubtedly indicate a high level of tax due. Since the CRA has made the net-worth assessments cover a number of years, the tax owing for each year will accumulate daily interest plus penalties at an alarming rate, further inflating the tax bill to astronomical proportions. The assessments may be inaccurate for many reasons, but the reverse onus of proof puts the burden on the taxpayer to disprove the Agency's findings. In the absence of such proof, or if the proof is not accepted, the CRA's assessment will stand.

Your Best Defence: Secret lifestyle audits are not usually initiated without cause. Accurate and timely submission of your tax returns, prepared by a credentialed and reputable accountant or tax adviser, is the best way to keep from being targeted for this type of investigation. Retain an experienced tax lawyer to submit a carefully prepared reconstruction of your income for the years in question (created under the auspices of lawyer-client privilege) that accurately represents your taxable income and legitimate expenses and deductions.

2. 1-800-SNITCH LINE

When: Any time an ex-spouse, colleague, business competitor, neighbour, friend, or anyone else in the world thinks you may "be up to something."

What: The Agency offers individuals the opportunity to provide information about any person or business they suspect of cheating on their taxes without revealing their own names. To quote an entry from the Enforcement and Disclosures section of the CRA website:

> If you have information about a suspected violation of any tax law, please contact the CRA Enforcement division nearest you.

Click on the link and there is a list of the district tax offices across Canada. Dial the number, give them the scoop, and investigations will be on the case with a net-worth assessment, a secret lifestyle assessment, an audit, or worse.

The Agency's Advantage: Thanks to the informant's phone call, the CRA now has a hot lead to pursue, complete with a road map to your home, your business, your cottage, your bank accounts, your offshore holdings, or anything else the informant may have revealed. An angry ex-spouse can be the most dangerous of informants, because he or she likely knows the darkest of your financial secrets—and might well be disposed to spill them all in an attack against you.

Danger to the Taxpayer: When the Agency is told where to look, and what to look for, it will quickly find the evidence it seeks, placing you in serious jeopardy of a criminal investigation and prosecution.

Your Best Defence: Know your enemies. Start with spouses, ex-spouses, neighbours, business partners, and creditors. If you are hiding any tax secrets, people in your life could turn against you at any time. Don't give them the chance to call the snitch line on you. If any of the relationships in your life suddenly goes sour, your best defence is to resolve your tax situation BEFORE your enemies call the CRA. In such cases, a lawyer-negotiated tax settlement is likely your safest route.

3. NON-ARM'S-LENGTH TRANSFERS OF PROPERTY

When: In some cases, knowing that a large tax bill will be due even before a tax return is filed, taxpayers will transfer property to a spouse, a relative, a business colleague, or even a friend, in an attempt to deplete assets and prevent the CRA from seizing the property to collect on the tax debt.

What: Section 160 of the Income Tax Act was put in place to prevent a taxpayer from avoiding payment of outstanding taxes by transferring property in a non-arm's-length transaction for less than the receipt of fair market value. If the tax debtor transfers property in a non-arm's-length transaction during or after the taxation year in which the tax debtor is liable, the transferor and the transferee can be jointly and severally liable for payment of the tax debtor's liability to the Agency. This liability can apply even if no assessment was made against the tax debtor.

The Agency's Advantage: Under Section 160, if the transfer is made during the taxation year in which the tax is owed or at any time thereafter, the recipient of the property (the transferee) can be held personally responsible for all or part of the tax owed by the transferor up to the shortfall for the fair market value paid for the property.

Danger to the Taxpayer: There is no time limitation on the CRA's right to assess the transferee for the tax owing. Spouses may be divorced or widowed. Business partners may long since have dissolved their ties. Friends may have gone their separate ways. Notwithstanding any or all of the above, the tax liability remains.

A TAX NIGHTMARE TWO WAYS

1. Jim and Jane are married, but their house has always been in his name only. Jim transfers ownership to Jane in March, six weeks before his tax return for the previous calendar year is filed. He owes the CRA $100,000 but does not have

the cash to pay. The tax debt remains outstanding. A year later, thinking they're safe from the CRA, Jane transfers the house back to him. Three years later, Jane receives a tax assessment for Jim's still outstanding tax debt. Consultation with her accountant and, ultimately, a tax lawyer, reveal that Jane, as the recipient of the transfer at the time the tax was owed, remains liable for the tax debt under Section 160, even though she no longer owns the home.

2. Before marriage, Rob transfers to Heather what will become their matrimonial home under a prenuptial agreement. At that time, Rob has taxes due. A few years into the marriage, Rob becomes ill and cannot carry on with the business that is the sole source of the family's income. All the financial resources Heather brought into the marriage—considerably more than the value of the home—are spent keeping them afloat. Ultimately, Rob declares bankruptcy and is granted an absolute discharge. Time passes, and Rob and Heather divorce. Heather mortgages the home to satisfy Rob's rights under family law to half of the matrimonial home's fair market value. Then Section 160 comes back to haunt Heather. Seeking repayment of Rob's unpaid tax debt, the CRA assesses Heather for the home's fair market value at the time of transfer, even though she was unaware of Rob's tax liability, even though half of the home's value has been paid to Rob under the family law rules, and even though her only resource is the mortgaged home.

Your Best Defence: Forewarned is forearmed. Property can be transferred safely from one spouse to the other when there is no outstanding tax debt. Thereafter, if the first spouse has unpaid tax, the CRA will be unable to assess the spouse who owns the property for payment. When one half of a couple is the sole owner of a business, and the other spouse has no interests or responsibilities in the business, this strategy can make the home a CRA-proof asset.

4. YOUR ACCOUNTANT—THE AGENCY'S CAPTIVE WITNESS AGAINST YOU

When: If the CRA wishes to look deeper into your financial activities

What: Accountants and tax preparers are required to have the taxpayer complete and sign forms disclosing any foreign assets for which you paid in excess of $100,000, or any accounts holding balances in excess of $100,000. The forms also ask if you, or a trust in which you have an interest, own shares in a foreign company, or if you ever made a loan or a gift to a foreign trust or company.

Tax advisers also require you to sign a declaration stating that "*You are not aware of any illegal or possibly illegal acts related to your income or investments, including any deductions for expenses, for which you have not disclosed to me all facts related thereto.*"

Refuse to sign the waiver and the accountant will decline to prepare and file your tax return. But we have to ask why anyone of sound mind would reveal an illegal activity without the protection of lawyer-client confidentiality—a privilege most certainly NOT extended to accounting professionals.

The Agency's Advantage: Penalties for failure to file the necessary reporting forms are severe. If an accountant or other tax preparer is aware that a client is not reporting all sources of income, or that income is derived from an illegal source, yet still continues to act as the client's representative, he or she can be fined by the CRA and/or have their privilege to electronically file tax returns revoked.

Danger to the Taxpayer: Accountants and tax preparers do not have the legal privilege of lawyer-client confidentiality. If the Agency demands information about you and your finances, accountants are required to comply. They may even be called by the Agency to testify against you in an investigation. If your accountant knows your secrets—eventually the CRA will, too.

Your Best Defence: Utilize your accountant or tax adviser in the role for which he or she is best suited—to prepare and file your tax return. Any other interaction with the CRA—disputes, responses to assessments, audits, investigations, and collection action, even catching up on unfiled tax returns that are more than one year in arrears—should be managed by an experienced tax lawyer who can protect your financial information with lawyer-client privilege and negotiate on your behalf without exposing your secrets.

5. FORMAL REQUIREMENT FOR INFORMATION

When: If the Agency has suspicions—founded or unfounded—about the integrity of your reporting of income and taxable gains.

What: The CRA has the power to "require" information from any person. The demand can be for something as simple as a tax return, or as complicated as a full disclosure of an entire office full of documents. The Agency can demand the cooperation of an accountant, a tax preparer, a bank manager, stockbroker, spouse, neighbour, business partner—anyone who has any relationship of any kind to the taxpayer. This includes the power to enforce any requests to provide written answers to questions.

The Agency's Advantage: The requirement for information is a formal matter, with a hearing officer appointed through application to the

Tax Court of Canada. When appointed, the hearing officer has the right to call witnesses and require them to give evidence under oath and to produce documents. The inquiry can be used to accumulate evidence for possible penalties or criminal prosecution.

Danger to the Taxpayer: Anyone called as a witness will be required, under oath, to truthfully reveal what they know about your financial situation. Your accountant is particularly vulnerable and can easily be become the CRA's star witness against you.

Your Best Defence: Having proper legal representation is crucial to the protection of your rights of privacy. A experienced tax lawyer will be able to recommend a strategy to mitigate the information that may come to light in a hearing, and may even be able to step between the CRA and your accountant to use the principle of lawyer-client privilege to prevent your accountant from having to testify—or at least reduce the amount of information that must be provided, protecting as much of your financial privacy as possible.

6. SEARCH AND SEIZURE

When: The CRA requires documentation or other evidence in the course of an investigation, and does not trust you to voluntarily provide complete answers to their questions.

What: A search and seizure warrant gives the CRA permission to enter any premises to search for and seize any document or thing. This usually includes computers, where even documents and electronic messages that have been erased still can be reconstructed from their imprint on the hard drive.

The Agency's Advantage: The warrant can be obtained through an *ex parte* (without notice to the taxpayer) application to a judge. Senior-level agents carry search warrants with them that can be used as required.

Danger to the Taxpayer: Caught unawares, you will have no opportunity to select what documents are revealed to the Agency. Tax agents may be investigating a particular matter, and then discover new evidence in your files—perhaps in an email sent to a colleague and then deleted—that permits the Agency to expand the investigation to encompass new areas.

Your Best Defence: When confronted by search and seizure, compliance is your only option. Politely ask for an opportunity to contact legal counsel immediately. The authorities may or may not permit this. You may not at this time deny the authorities access to your home or office, or impede their seizure efforts. As soon as possible, have your tax lawyer review the warrant(s) to assess the legality of the search and seizure. Any irregularities can be addressed as part of your defence in court.

7. GARNISHMENTS, SEIZURE OF ASSETS, PROPERTY LIENS

When: After a tax assessment has been mailed to a taxpayer, payment in full is due immediately. If no payment, or payment arrangement, is made and no objection or appeal is filed, the CRA can take immediate action to collect the tax debt. If the CRA has reason to suspect the assets are in jeopardy—that you may sell, mortgage, or transfer them to someone else—it may decide to make the seizure before the assessment is issued.

What:
• Garnishment of wages

- Third-party demands on suppliers from whom receivables are due to you
- Seizure of government funds due to you, such as GST tax credits, income tax refunds, old age security, and Canada Pension Plan benefits
- Seizure of your bank accounts and seizure and sale of your assets or goods
- Registration of liens on your real property

The Agency may, at its discretion, implement any or all of these to enforce payment of or collect on the tax debt owing.

The Agency's Advantage: The CRA is not required to notify you in advance of its intention to exercise any of these collection options. It thus has the element of surprise on its side, preventing you from taking pre-emptive action to protect your financial position. By diverting your cash and/or seizing control of your bank accounts and assets, the CRA is forcing you to pay off your tax debt.

Danger to the Taxpayer: Your bank, your employer, and your business customers are by law compelled to comply with the Agency's demands. You can be taken totally unawares. Perhaps you go to renew your mortgage and find that the bank won't touch you because the CRA has registered a lien against the property. Or, even worse, you go the ATM to get money for groceries and discover that the CRA has frozen your accounts and you cannot access a dime. You won't be able to feed your children, put gas in the car, pay the mortgage, or do anything else until you negotiate with the Agency to release your accounts. A wage garnishment forces your employer to remit whatever is demanded to the government, often leaving you without enough money to live on. And, if your business customers are compelled to pay your receivables directly to the CRA, the credibility your business has lost might never be regained.

Your Best Defence: You will need to file an offer to settle your debt, or arrange an installment payment agreement you can live with in order to restore access to your cash flow and/or release of your property. While you can undertake this on your own, it is safer to retain the services of an experienced tax lawyer to ensure that the agreement with the CRA is binding and will not be retracted at the whim of the tax office.

Note: While a 10-year limitation period with respect to outstanding tax debts has become standard practice, the Agency has devised ways to deal with outstanding, uncollected tax debts over a longer period of time.

8. OPPOSITION TO BANKRUPTCY DISCHARGE

When: The taxpayer seeks to avoid payment of a tax debt by declaring bankruptcy.

What: As a major creditor, the CRA may choose to oppose a taxpayer's discharge from bankruptcy.

The Agency's Advantage: The CRA can be instrumental in rejecting a reasonable creditor proposal to repay debt. Depending on the magnitude of the debt, this may push the taxpayer into the powerless state of bankruptcy. However, instead of writing off the tax debt, after the bankruptcy the CRA can then seek a conditional order from the Court for additional payments, prolonging the term of the bankruptcy before discharge. This permits the Agency to collect more of the tax debt over several years.

Danger to the Taxpayer: Your application for bankruptcy can trigger an investigation of your tax situation—especially if this is not your first bankruptcy. If the CRA discovers you are not declaring all your revenue (i.e., if tax evasion was involved), or if it is able to substantiate a large lifestyle assessment against you, a criminal charge can be laid against you for tax evasion. Thumbing your nose at government by going bankrupt can lead them to want to make an example of you and start a criminal prosecution. If the CRA proves its case, and you are convicted, the judge will levy a fine. If you can't pay, you can be sent to jail for up to two years. Serving jail time does not discharge your civil tax debt.

Your Best Defence: If your tax debt is truly pushing you into insolvency, rather than rushing headlong into a bankruptcy, work out a sound strategy for a creditor proposal. An experienced tax lawyer can help you anticipate the Agency's response, as well as the most likely response from other creditors, and then help you negotiate a solution that will protect your interests as much as possible.

9. EXCHANGE OF INFORMATION BETWEEN FEDERAL AND PROVINCIAL TAX AUTHORITIES

When: Routine and ongoing.

What: The federal tax authority (the CRA) has agreements with all the provinces (except Quebec, which has its own tax system) to collect personal and, in some cases, corporate taxes. Under such agreements, each province must provide the CRA with information on any person subject to tax in the province, including any real estate transactions or valuations. In return, the CRA provides information to provincial tax authorities with respect to assessments, collections, and payments. There is a special arrangement with Quebec with respect to the sharing of information. Quebec also collects and administers the GST in that province on behalf of the federal tax authority, and reports any issues in collecting this tax. Quebec also has a formal working relationship with its own provincial police to share information on possible tax cheats.

The Agency's Advantage: The federal tax authority is able to harness the provincial tax departments as sources of information about your financial and tax status.

Danger to the Taxpayer: Tax liabilities or non-compliance at the provincial level can trigger suspicions at the federal level, leading to an investigation. Corporations and businesses face additional risk at the provincial level. For instance, for Ontario-registered businesses, the provincial Minister of Finance will cancel the corporate charters of companies that fail to file returns. This could lead to seizure of corporate assets by the Crown, loss of insurance coverage, and loss of the right to claim tax losses. Companies that owe tax will be required to pay a late-filing penalty, and their directors may be prosecuted and fined on a daily basis.

These aggressive measures have been implemented in response to large-scale non-compliance, as expressed in a CBC News online article dated February 10, 2003, which stated that "half of the 700,000 companies registered in Ontario failed to submit a tax return in 2001."

Your Best Defence: Filing personal and business/corporate tax returns on time is the best defence. If you are behind in your filings or have outstanding tax debt, experienced legal tax counsel will be vital to negotiating a settlement at the federal level, or the provincial level, or both, to forestall deregistration, seizure of assets, penalties, and prosecution.

10. FOREIGN TAX TREATIES

When: Canadians who live in the US or elsewhere abroad, and owe money to the CRA in Canada.

What: Canada has a network of bilateral tax treaties under which it provides information to foreign governments, on a reciprocal basis, for the administration and enforcement of domestic laws concerning taxes of any kind. Each contracting state agrees to use its powers to gather the requested information and remit it even though the other state may not need such information for its own tax purposes. This includes information held by banks or other financial institutions in its jurisdiction.

The Agency's Advantage: Tax authorities can step in and seize bank accounts or property in their jurisdiction pending settlement of a tax debt in Canada. Banks and financial institutions in foreign jurisdictions also can be compelled by the Canada Revenue Agency to provide details of taxpayers' transactions, and Canadian banks with ties to offshore tax havens risk losing their licences if they do not comply with these requests.

Danger to the Taxpayer: The CRA will call upon its foreign counterparts to seize your assets and property abroad at the same time it seizes your assets and property in Canada. Even more dangerous than this, a recent Supreme Court of Canada ruling declared that Canadians accused of crimes are not protected by the Charter of Rights and Freedoms while being investigated by either Canadian or foreign authorities (*Regina vs. Hape*, 2007). This means evidence recovered outside of Canada by a foreign enforcement agency, working with the RCMP, is exempt from the inadmissibility rules that would govern an unreasonable search and seizure by police forces in Canada.

In one case, after an investigation of his offshore trust company in the Turks and Caicos Islands, a Canadian businessman was convicted of laundering the proceeds of drug money. The defendant argued that the

Supreme Court should overturn his conviction on the grounds that the RCMP had violated his Charter rights against unreasonable search and seizure when they conducted covert raids of his company, downloaded files from his computers, and seized boxes of records. The Supreme Court ruled that the Charter did not apply in this case because the Turks and Caicos police, not the RCMP, were in charge of the investigation on the islands. This landmark ruling set a precedent whereby Canadians are not guaranteed the protection of their Charter rights when they are the targets of criminal investigations in foreign jurisdictions.

This ruling casts serious doubt on the protection of tax havens for Canadians seeking to avoid taxation by hiding money offshore.

Your Best Defence: In order to secure release of your foreign assets, you will need to negotiate with Canadian tax authorities and reach a settlement of your Canadian tax debts. You should work with a tax lawyer to ensure that you are protected from prosecution and your non-declared foreign assets are legitimized.

The following countries have tax treaties with Canada

Algeria	Dominican	Jordan	Pakistan	Switzerland
Argentina	Republic	Kazakhstan	Papua New	Tanzania
Armenia	Ecuador	Kenya	Guinea	Thailand
Australia	Egypt	Kuwait	Peru	Trinidad and
Austria	Estonia	Kyrgyzstan	Philippines	Tobago
Azerbaijan	Finland	Latvia	Poland	Tunisia
Bangladesh	France	Lithuania	Portugal	Ukraine
Barbados	Germany	Luxembourg	Romania	United Arab
Belgium	Guyana	Malaysia	Russia	Emirates
Brazil	Hungary	Malta	Senegal	United
Bulgaria	Iceland	Mexico	Singapore	Kingdom
Cameroon	India	Moldova	Slovak	United
Chile	Indonesia	Mongolia	Republic	States
China (PRC)*	Ireland	Morocco	Slovenia	Uzbekistan
Croatia	Israel	Netherlands	South Africa	Venezuela
Cyprus	Italy	New Zealand	South Korea	Vietnam
Czech	Ivory Coast	Nigeria	Spain	Zambia
Republic	Jamaica	Norway	Sri Lanka	Zimbabwe
Denmark	Japan	Oman	Sweden	

* The treaty Canada has with China does not apply to Hong Kong.

TAXPAYER TAE KWON DO

Lessons from the Martial Arts to Keep the Agency at Bay

Adapted from the fundamentals of tae kwon do and other martial arts, these strategies can be deployed both defensively and offensively to help you hold your own against the Agency.

- **Utilize your opponent to increase your strength and obtain the advantage.** In tae kwon do, it is sometimes necessary to deflect a strike and to counterstrike. It is important to try to keep your opponent off balance to decrease your opponent's effectiveness. A tax auditor will likely want to catch you unprepared and will ask you selected questions to try to obtain an advantage. If these queries are deflected to your tax lawyer, you have minimized the Agency's strength.
- **Focus on your opponent and never turn your back.** Audits and tax assessments usually require an enormous amount of your focus and time; the Agency knows exactly what it wants. In tae kwon do, you never turn your back on your opponent. Never let a tax auditor meet alone with members of your staff. Remember: the Agency believes that you are guilty before starting an audit.
- **Keep your opponent at a distance.** In tae kwon do, keeping the proper distance is imperative. If the Agency gets too close to you, you will be put at a disadvantage.
- **Do not let your opponent invade your space.** In martial arts, there is a hypothetical space between you and your opponent. This space allows you time to properly defend yourself. Allowing a tax auditor into your boardroom while you are operating your business does not grant you the space or the time to

defend yourself if the auditor decides to make an offensive move. Do not let the auditor enter your home or place of business. If this cannot be avoided, insist that your legal counsel be in attendance.

- **Understand your opponent.** In martial arts, knowing and understanding your opponent is vital. If you don't have enough knowledge of the taxman, retain someone who does.

- **Anticipate your opponent's moves.** In martial arts, you must anticipate your opponent's moves. In tax audits, you must anticipate the Agency's next move.

8

THE RIGHT PROFESSIONAL FOR THE RIGHT TASK

Since this book is about problems that taxpayers can encounter with the CRA, it is, indeed, all about tax. More specifically, it is about tax law, because the CRA is the authority that administers the tax laws of Canada. Thus, in the context of this book, tax pertains to law.

LAWYER-CLIENT PRIVILEGE AND WHY IT MATTERS WHEN YOU ARE DEALING WITH THE AGENCY

The "lawyer-client privilege" of confidentiality means that a tax lawyer has the right to refuse to disclose an oral or written communication on the grounds that it has passed between a client and his lawyers in professional confidence. The right to complete privacy of communications is the cornerstone of the legal profession. This legal privilege forbids disclosure of communications made between lawyer and client for the purpose of seeking legal advice during the course of any legal proceeding such as an amnesty negotiation, audit, tax appeal, or criminal or civil court case.

J. C. McRuer, a prominent Canadian jurist, justified the lawyer's legal right to keep client information secret as follows: "Without solicitor-client privilege the whole structure of our adversary system of administering justice would collapse, for the object of that system is that the rights of all persons shall be submitted with equal force to the courts. If a lawyer is to give useful service to his client, he must be free to learn the whole of his client's case. The basis of the privilege between solicitor and client is . . . that confidentiality is necessary to insure that the public, with safety, may substitute legal advisers in their place instead of having to conduct their own cases and advise themselves."

ACCOUNTANTS CANNOT PROTECT YOUR PRIVACY

Accountants and other advisers do not have the safeguard of lawyer-client privilege. Thus, there is no legal protection for an accountant's working papers or any tax advice that may have been given. As well, the CRA makes extensive use of Section 231(2) of the Income Tax Act, which relates to third-party information demands. By this law, accountants can be forced to assist the Agency and even testify against their own client(s).

This rule has been tested in many court cases, one of which, BDO Dunwoody (Tower), was decided by the Federal Court of Appeal (2003). At issue was whether or not certain materials prepared by the accounting firm BDO Dunwoody to provide tax advice were privileged or could be used by the Canada Revenue Agency against BDO Dunwoody's clients.

The BDO Dunwoody clients argued in court that, had they known that BDO's tax advice could only be shielded by lawyer-client privilege, they would not have discussed these matters with their accountants.

The court decided that "lawyers are legally and ethically required to uphold and protect the public interest in the administration of justice. In contrast, accountants are not so bound. Nor do they provide legal advice; to do so would constitute a breach of provincial and territorial laws governing the legal professions. No overriding policy consideration exists so as to elevate the advice given by tax accountants to the level of solicitor-client privilege."

Under Section 231(2), accountants and other advisers are personally subject to pay heavy third-party penalties. Any adviser who counsels a taxpayer to make a false statement in a tax return is potentially liable. It can also cover gross negligence. Accountants who know their clients have undeclared offshore income must advise them to file foreign-reporting forms. Large fines are payable for failure to do so.

If the accountant has kept detailed notes of such discussions with clients, action could be taken against the accountant, putting him or her in a potential conflict-of-interest situation. If the client gets into a fight with the Agency or provincial tax authority, it puts their accountant in a difficult position.

Only Quebec-based accountants can see a faint light at the end of this rather dark tunnel. Under provincial law they have been given a restricted right of professional confidentiality, but only when dealing with the MRQ (Ministère du Revenu du Québec). The Québec Charter of Human Rights and Freedoms provides that a person bound to professional secrecy by law cannot disclose confidential information revealed in a professional capacity unless authorized to do so by the person who gave such information, or by a provision of the law. The big problem is that it does not apply to any negotiations accountants in Québec try to do for clients with the CRA, since it is an arm of the federal government. Moreover, if the federal tax authorities lay criminal charges, the Quebec accountant will be unable to hold to the privilege of confidentiality.

YOUR POWER TAX TEAM

As the cases in this book demonstrate, an experienced tax lawyer is essential in any situation in which a taxpayer is in opposition to the CRA or a provincial tax authority.

This should not be construed to suggest that an accountant—particularly an accountant who has been instrumental in the preparation and filing of your financial records and tax returns for many years—is *persona non grata*. Accountants can be an essential part of your tax team, but they must be deployed properly and carefully in the course of negotiation for an amnesty or tax relief settlement, especially in situations where criminal liability might apply.

Tax lawyers can, when required, hire either the client's own accountant or an outside accountant to provide or recreate the financial information required to negotiate a settlement. It all comes down the principle of **work product privilege**. The accountant, when working in this capacity for and under the auspices of the tax lawyer, is fully protected by the lawyer's legal privilege to maintain client confidentiality. This protects the accountant from being called to bear witness against the client. Moreover, since the accountant is already familiar with the client's financial and tax situation, the lawyers are provided with accurate information upon which to base submissions to the CRA. In these situations, the accountant's fees will be paid by the lawyers, as part of the disbursements charged to the client.

There are three caveats to working in such a "tax team" alliance. First, if the client's own accountant is used to do the accounting work and settlement cannot be reached with the CRA, the accountant, because of third-party liability rules, may no longer be able to represent the client in this case. The accountant may have had previous specific knowledge of the client's case, which may include deliberate tax evasion, and by law would be required to reveal that knowledge upon demand. For this reason, many clients prefer to use an outside accountant working under the tax lawyer to complete the financial reporting aspects of amnesty or equity submissions.

Second, the tax lawyer must solely be in charge of the contact and negotiations with the CRA, and cannot be used by the accountant as a rubber stamp. If the accountant manages the negotiations, the protection of lawyer-client confidentiality is forfeit, and the Agency can force the accountant to testify against the client.

And finally, if the accountant is also qualified as a lawyer and chooses to fulfill the roles of both negotiating lawyer and accountant, the work performed as an accountant cannot be protected by lawyer-client confidentiality. This leaves a big opening for the CRA to subpoena financial records and call the accountant-lawyer to bear witness against the client. In this case, the dual qualification can be more of a liability than an asset.

WHEN IS AN ACCOUNTANT NOT A SUBSTITUTE FOR A TAX LAWYER?

Some years ago, a field audit was begun by the Agency into the affairs of a corporation that operated a restaurant. An audit letter was forwarded to the principal shareholder, who sent it to his accountants for advice.

The CRA auditor met with the shareholder, Mr. X, and an associate of the accounting firm. The auditor also toured the business premises and asked detailed questions about the operations. Then the CRA auditor transferred any records not already in the possession of the accounting firm to the accounting firm's office, where he conducted an examination of several years of financial records.

Mr. X had yet to contact legal counsel. This was a tax matter, he believed, and it would be well-handled by his accounting firm.

He was proven wrong when, at the conclusion of the office review, the CRA auditor removed the boxes of financial records from the offices of his accountants without consent, and without completing the mandatory "Borrowed Records" form.

Still without the protection of legal counsel, the shareholder and his accountants participated in further discussions with the CRA auditor that later proved critical to the auditor's recommendation for an investigation in order to build a case for criminal charges.

Meanwhile, discussions with the accountants continued. On the auditor's recommendation, the Agency's Investigations officers retroactively obtained a search and seizure order, which now gave the CRA legal permission to seize the boxes of documents that had previously been removed from the accountant's premises, and which were in the possession of the CRA. Under the authority of this order, the home of the shareholder, his place of business, and the accounting firm's offices were also searched.

Several months later, criminal charges were brought against the corporation and the principal shareholder, as well as against some associates of the accounting firm for allegedly conspiring with, counseling, and aiding and abetting the corporation and its principals. Only at this stage did the shareholder retain legal counsel.

Ultimately, all criminal charges were dropped, in return for a guilty plea plus a heavy civil fine. We can only wonder if Mr. X still believes he was right to leave such a serious and escalating matter in the hands of the accountants who were themselves eventually charged as co-conspirators.

TAX AMNESTY AND TAXPAYER RELIEF

The Canadian tax system is one of the most complicated in the world, and consequently also one of the most expensive to administer. The cost of tax collection is very high, and the more steps needed to finally secure the tax debt owing, the higher the cost to our government, and ultimately, you, the taxpayer. Provisions for tax amnesty and tax equity relief are relatively inexpensive methods of collecting tax, since the bulk of the effort is expended by the taxpayer and his lawyers in negotiating a safe and manageable way for the taxpayer to become tax compliant. If the tax lawyer properly handles negotiations and a reasonable settlement can be achieved, it's a win-win situation for both sides.

It is important to note that the granting of tax relief, in either an amnesty application or an equity submission, is discretionary and is negotiated on a case-by-case basis. A tax lawyer offers the greatest leverage in dealing with the CRA for a number of reasons. In an amnesty situation, the lawyer can protect the anonymity of the taxpayer until such time as an acceptable, written agreement has been reached. As an example, in situations where tax has not been declared or paid for a long time, an important part of the discussion is the number of years that will be subject to tax. Often there are reasons why some years should be excluded, and this must be brought forward during ongoing talks with the official charged with making the decision to refuse or grant the amnesty. The Agency has restricted the amnesty program to no more than 10 years, which makes the confidentiality privilege of the lawyer even more vital. Once an acceptable agreement has been reached, the taxpayer's name is disclosed, tax returns are filed, and taxes owing are paid.

Negotiations for taxpayer relief begin only when the CRA and the taxpayer are already in discussion, dispute, or negotiation over tax owing. In this situation, lawyer-client privilege grants the tax lawyer the ability to reveal only what is necessary or relevant to the particular tax matter under discussion.

In an amnesty situation, the lawyer can protect the anonymity of the taxpayer.

If the initial submission is declined, the tax lawyer already has prepared the groundwork to take the case to other levels, including the courts. In the event that, after an amnesty or equity settlement has been reached, the client does not have sufficient funds to discharge the tax owing, a satisfactory arrangement can usually be worked out later with collections officers.

In serious financial hardship cases, where the client has little or no money or assets, it may be necessary to assist in arranging for a consumer proposal or other creditor negotiation.

When Not to Talk to Your Accountant

- If you receive a Notice of Audit letter and are required to respond to questions, your accountant may ask you questions about your finances. Be careful how you answer. Any information you share with your accountant is compellable by the CRA.
- During an audit stage, particularly if there is some suspicion of wrongdoing, you should speak with your accountant only on the advice of your tax lawyer.
- When accountants have used questionable methods and thus put themselves in a clear conflict-of-interest position. The accountants should advise you about this immediately so that you can seek legal advice.
- Your accountant should not act as an advocate for you with the tax auditors or investigators, since he or she may be compelled to provide damaging documentary or other information against you. No one can be both advocate for and potential informant against a client.

When Not to Let Your Accountant Talk to the CRA

- If you are in an adversarial dispute with the CRA
- If you have received a Notice of Reassessment that you wish to appeal
- If you receive a Notice of Audit
- If you receive a Demand to File Notice going back further than the most current tax year
- If the CRA asks to review your company books, or see tax returns for more than the current tax year
- If you have reason to suspect you are under investigation by the CRA

When Not to Talk to the CRA on Your Own

- If an agent suddenly arrives at your door. You are entitled to decline to speak with the agent. If the agent does not have a search warrant, you are not obliged to admit the agent to your home of office. If the agent has a search warrant, you have no choice but to permit access as requested. Do not, however, answer questions, and contact your legal counsel as quickly as possible.
- If an agent calls and starts asking questions about your tax return or other financial matters
- If your bank accounts/assets are seized by the CRA
- If your clients are served with Third-Party Payment letters
- If you wish to dispute a substantial reassessment
- If you receive a Notice of Audit
- If you owe a large amount of tax and cannot pay. An appropriate advocate, preferably a tax lawyer, is more likely to be successful in approaching the CRA to negotiate a payment schedule. Trying to go it alone and then being turned down will make it harder for your advocate to succeed on your behalf.

- If you receive a notice to file for more than the current tax year
- If you are contacted by the CRA when you know you are delinquent in filing tax returns for more than the current tax year, or you have deliberately not reported all your income on your tax return(s)
- If you have not been remitting source deductions/GST/HST, or other trust monies, and the CRA calls looking for the money
- If you are notified that you are under investigation, or are charged with criminal tax evasion

In all of the above scenarios, there is danger in even speaking with the CRA without the protection of legal counsel. The agency may try to trap you into revealing information that can later be used against you. Consult an experienced tax lawyer, who can speak to the CRA on your behalf.

9

BEFORE THE AGENCY COMES: THE AMNESTY ALTERNATIVE

A clean confession, combined with a promise to never commit the sin again, when offered before one who has the right to receive it, is the purest type of repentance.

—*The Mahatma Mohandas Karamchand Gandhi*

(1869–1948)

The CRA has created an amnesty program to entice tax evaders and tax non-filers to identify themselves and get back into the system. It wants them to report all the income on which tax was evaded, and file all the tax returns in arrears. In return for this voluntary admission of tax delinquency, the taxpayers will be granted "forgiveness" and allowed to negotiate a settlement of their tax arrears.

The CRA presents this amnesty as its Voluntary Disclosures Program (VDP) and promotes it to taxpayers on its website and through accountants and other tax advisers.

The rules to qualify for the VDP are deceptively simple:

- The tax evader must not be already under investigation by the Agency.
- The tax evader has to give a full and truthful statement of the facts and the amounts involved in the tax evasion and not try to "cook the books." (This includes voluntarily answering any question the Agency asks about your income and financial situation.)
- The tax evader must be subject to a penalty.
- Any forgiveness and negotiated settlement will not include a current tax year.
- The maximum period for which civil and criminal penalties can be waived is 10 years.

The offer to come clean simply by approaching the CRA on your own may be appealing to the repentant tax evader. But beneath the surface lie a number of legal traps.

SELF-INCRIMINATION

"Voluntary" is the operative word in the VDP. By voluntarily disclosing your tax delinquency and the details thereof, you are also voluntarily giving up your Charter rights against self-incrimination in admitting to the offence of failure to file and/or not reporting all your income. Thus you stand, self-confessed of an offence punishable in the criminal courts, having provided the Crown with detailed evidence that can be used to convict you because, as evidence, it was disclosed voluntarily and is therefore admissible in a court of law.

The CRA's "tax police" handle the VDP. Remember that the "tax police" are the agents who undertake net-worth assessments, lifestyle audits, and other "secret" investigations to discover evidence of tax evasion. They are the agents you will face in the courtroom if you are charged with criminal tax evasion.

Does it sound like a wise move to hand over your tax secrets to these people?

The Agency believes that Canadians will trust it with their tax secrets, and actively encourages those who have not been tax compliant to come forward on their own or through their accountant. The invitation as reprinted from the CRA website, reads as follows:

> The Voluntary Disclosures Program (VDP) allows taxpayers to come forward and correct inaccurate or incomplete information or disclose material they did not report during previous dealings with the CRA, without penalty or prosecution.

The impression it wishes to convey is that the Agency is sympathetic and will listen to your story and then forgive. No mention is made that you may be audited at any time in the future, and that the audit may include the years for which you have been "forgiven," or that, based on your revelations, the Agency may undertake its own net-worth assessment to validate your information. Either of these events can trigger a criminal investigation and lead to prosecution for criminal tax evasion. In the event you are not accepted for a VDP tax settlement, you also can be prosecuted for criminal tax evasion, and everything you have revealed is available to be used against you at your trial.

These very real dangers transform what is presented as a simple "reporting" correction into a legal minefield with serious consequences.

Not understanding these issues, many tax delinquents ask their accountant to assist them in coming forward under the VDP. If the exercise were simply a matter of reporting income and filing tax returns, this would be an appropriate process. But the fundamental situation of a VDP is that of a delinquent taxpayer who is admitting to the commission of a criminal offence. You wouldn't ask an accountant to accompany you to the police to confess to fraud, or theft, or any other crime. You would want—and would ultimately be urged to accept—the protection and representation of legal counsel to protect your rights. Most importantly, your legal counsel would be able to protect you through lawyer-client privilege and could not be compelled to testify against you or reveal incriminating information about you to the authorities.

Accountants, regardless of the stature of their credentials, are not granted the right of client privilege and are therefore unable to protect your information from the Agency in the face of a subpoena or a formal request for information.

Would you want to have someone negotiating a tax settlement on your behalf to be in such a vulnerable position? He or she could turn into the Agency's star witness against you if anything goes wrong.

Tax lawyers understand that a taxpayer's Charter rights must be protected to the greatest possible extent, and that only a lawyer, with the confidentiality of lawyer-client privilege recognized, respected, and upheld in court, can provide this protection. Tax lawyers also recognize that while the VDP offers "forgiveness" to the tax delinquent, the client must be protected from criminal and civil penalties during the settlement negotiations.

A lawyer-negotiated amnesty settlement leverages the opportunity of the CRA's VDP to come forward and remedy past tax omissions, but also provides the taxpayer with some specific legal protections not encompassed by this disclosure program.

 Accountants are not granted the right of client privilege and are therefore unable to protect your information from the Agency.

The process starts with a no-name disclosure proposal to the Agency on a preliminary basis. If the Agency agrees that, based on the proposal, and provided disclosure is complete and accurate, the tax evader will be protected from criminal prosecution and civil and criminal penalties, it's on to the next stage. Then the tax lawyer will proceed, on the tax delinquent's behalf, to reveal his or her identity and negotiate a settlement of taxes owing and a reduction (or if possible, a waiver) of accrued interest. Once the lawyer has provided a full disclosure of the income for the tax years involved in the amnesty, and once the CRA has reviewed these tax returns and accepted them as accurate, the lawyer is able to finalize a binding tax settlement. If the disclosure complies with the rules, the Agency normally will not reopen those tax years for audit, reassessment, or criminal investigation in the future. However, if at some time in the future the CRA finds evidence that you were not completely honest in your disclosure, it always has the right to review your files and withdraw the amnesty granted.

If you haven't been filing tax returns, or have been misrepresenting your taxable income, or hiding assets, seeking amnesty with the help of an experienced tax lawyer is the only safe way to approach the Agency to resolve the situation.

TAX AMNESTY FAQS

What makes tax amnesty legally possible?
Under the provisions of the Income Tax and the Excise Tax acts, the Agency has the discretionary right to cancel civil and criminal penalties for failure to file and tax evasion as part of a negotiated settlement of individual or corporate tax liability. Provincial authorities have similar discretionary powers. Federal and provincial compliance officials also have the authority to waive or reduce outstanding interest.

What types of tax delinquency can be resolved through amnesty?
Under the federal VDP, situations that can be redressed by negotiating
a tax settlement include

- not filing personal returns
- not filing corporate or business returns
- not filing GST/HST returns
- failing to remit source deductions or the GST/HST
- failing to report all income
- claiming ineligible expenses
- failing to file correct customs accounting information

Can I negotiate an amnesty without a lawyer?
Under the VDP, you can approach the CRA on your own or through an
accountant or any other representative. You will be required to disclose
your identity and the details of your situation. You will not be able to
protect your information from being used against you in the future.

What if my application for amnesty is not accepted?
A tax lawyer will, in this situation, most likely request judicial review
of the decision to deny or partially deny a requested amnesty. (This
is another reason why you really want to have a tax lawyer represent
you in an amnesty application. An accountant usually does not have
the specific training or qualifications to make the necessary application to the federal court, and would have to enlist the assistance of a
lawyer at this stage.)

How many years can I wait before I come forward for an amnesty?
You can wait for as long as you wish. The longer you wait, however,
the greater the chance the Agency will find you first, which will make
you ineligible. It's also important to remember that, as of the time of
this writing, amnesty will be granted only for the most recent 10 years
of filing. If you wish to seek an amnesty, it is wise to do so before the

delinquent period exceeds 10 years. It is possible to resolve cases involving more than 10 years of unreported income, but the negotiations are extremely delicate. We have had success in such cases.

Can I negotiate an amnesty to wipe out all the tax owing?
No. An amnesty negotiation gives you the chance to make an honest declaration and pay the tax fairly due on your income. You may negotiate for the fairest possible assessment of tax owing, and may request a waiver of penalties and a reduction of the interest on the taxes due.

What if I can't pay the tax I owe after my amnesty is negotiated?
The Agency can revoke your tax amnesty if you do not pay the tax you owe, exposing you to penalties and prosecution. If you cannot pay immediately, we would recommend that you negotiate a payment schedule with the Agency, or try to borrow the money, or both. Your tax lawyer can help you negotiate payment arrangements.

WHY TAXPAYERS NEED AN AMNESTY
PART I—UNFILED TAX RETURNS

PROFILE OF A NON-FILER

Often the tax evader is male, in his 30s or 40s, a battered survivor of a financially devastating divorce or business breakup, or both. He likely no longer owns a home, a car, or anything of real value. He probably lost his job in the debacle and has been working freelance for cash. His attitude to authorities, and especially taxes, is "screw you." It can take years for the

CRA to track him down, since he probably lives with buddies, or in his parent's home, or with a string of girlfriends. He comes to light when, several years down the road, he is offered a job with a great salary. Suddenly he's on the CRA's radar. They start sending him Demand to File notices, then an arbitrary assessment, then the Demand to Pay, and finally track him down by phone at the office. Scared, he comes to the tax lawyer with a box holding dozens of unopened CRA envelopes. Best guess on tax owing by that time (including penalties and interest)? Two hundred and fifty thousand dollars or more. Criminal prosecution is also a danger.

Some people don't file a tax return every year. More than you might think, in fact. According to a Ufile tax-filers poll, published in a March 2007 press release, 13% of all Canadians polled said they know someone who has not yet filed their tax return for the previous year.

How many more Canadians are afraid to admit that they haven't filed? It's not something that generally comes up in the course of a conversation. In Canada, we think of ourselves as reasonably law-abiding citizens with a strong social conscience; we accept the responsibility for paying taxes as one of the privileges of our lifestyle. The idea that someone we know would shirk his or her responsibility by not filing a tax return just isn't "cricket."

Why, then, do so many Canadians neglect to file a return every year? Some—the smallest percentage of the non-filers—mistakenly believe that they don't have to file when their employer automatically deducts their income tax, CPP, EI, and healthcare premiums at source. They're not expecting a refund. So why should they bother with the stress and strain involved, not to mention the expense of tax-filing software or the services of a tax preparer?

Most non-filers, however, are afraid to file. It's usually a behaviour that begins by default one year. There's a sickness, or a devastating personal issue, or some other legitimate reason why they were not able to file by the April 30 deadline. Rather than address the issue later in the year, they simply let it slide. Then, with one year unfiled, they're not sure what to do when the next April 30 rolls around. And the deadline slides by again . . . and again . . . and again. Then the non-filer is faced not only with unfiled tax returns, but also with the dilemma of the unpaid tax from each year.

LIVING AND WORKING IN THE US

Q: *I lived in the US from 2002–2006 and earned income there, but did not file an income tax return in the US. I didn't file a Canadian return in that time either. (I didn't have any Canadian income, although I did make some RRSP and GIC contributions.) What are my options?*

A: If you retained a home here in Canada, or kept substantial ties with this country, you could be considered a Canadian resident for tax purposes. If such is not the case, you would be wise to apply to the CRA's International Tax Division in Ottawa for a ruling on your residency status (and therefore your tax status). You will be in a better position if you do this before the CRA comes after you with a letter asking why you didn't file. A proper legal assessment of your situation is recommended before you take any action.

The other non-filer scenario is even simpler. The non-filer knows he or she doesn't have the money to pay the tax bill and so just doesn't file. Perhaps knowing for sure how much is owed when there is no money to pay is just too upsetting, so he or she doesn't even bother preparing a tax return. On it goes from year to year to year; no return is filed, and, even more dangerously, no tax is paid.

Whatever the scenario, the non-filer is soon hiding what has grown into a very large tax delinquency, and is most likely living in fear that any day now the Agency will come knocking on the door.

Here's a bitter memory from a small businessman who, after a serious business setback, found himself with no money for taxes after feeding and housing his family:

"I went six years without filing a tax return. And every day, every time someone walked into my office that I didn't know, my heart would start to beat faster, for fear that it was someone from the tax department finally coming after me."

If you're not filing taxes every year, the Agency will track you down one day. When it does, you can face charges of criminal tax evasion for not filing a tax return every year as required by Section 238(1) of the Income Tax Act, as follows:

Income Tax Provision 238(1)
- Failure to file return at required time and manner
- Failure of non-resident to notify Minister of sale of taxable Canadian property
- Failure to deduct or withhold tax
- Failure to keep proper books and records

Penalty: On summary conviction, a fine from $1,000 to $25,000 and imprisonment for up to 12 months.

How Long Will the CRA Let You Go?

That depends on a number of factors. But it's important to know that once you slide into non-filer status, it's in the Agency's best interest to let you stay "undetected" for a while. The CRA makes more money that way.

If you're within a year of the missed tax-filing deadline, you're still in a grey zone. You're late with your return and subject to a small late-filing penalty, plus the daily interest on your outstanding taxes. But criminal charges do not apply until you are more than one year late past the filing date and taxes are owed. Then you can be charged with criminal tax evasion, with a heavy criminal fine, plus civil penalties, plus daily interest on both the tax and the penalties.

There's a greater reward for the Agency if it lets you go unchallenged for several years. (Remember that, as an agent of the government, the Agency representatives' performances are judged on how much money they bring back for each hour spent in pursuit of a taxpayer.) Added to the financial incentive is the ease of conviction on a criminal tax-evasion charge for non-filing. An unfiled tax return is the proof in black and white of your crime. There is no grey area. You didn't file. You are guilty as charged. At that level, it's a tough charge to beat.

Once you slide into non-filer status, it's in the Agency's best interest to let you stay "undetected" for a while.

Canadians find it hard to accept that the simple "oversight" of not filing a tax return is a criminal offence. They also don't believe that, if they are charged, they will be arraigned and tried in criminal court, along with alleged murderers, rapists, thieves, and thugs. Thus, they let unfiled tax returns add up, not knowing how to get safely back into the system, gambling that somehow the Agency won't find them.

It's a risky gamble. Fortunately, an amnesty offers a legal remedy to the situation.

THE CASE OF THE CARELESS PHOTOGRAPHER

Here's an extreme example from our files, where a serial non-filer literally was kept out of jail by an amnesty settlement.

Muriel was a photographer. That was her business and her sole source of income. She hadn't filed a tax return for 26 years. The sums involved were not large, but if the Agency ever found her out, the penalties and interest would add up to a total that she would have no hope of ever paying. It would force her into bankruptcy. She could also be charged with criminal tax evasion for the years of not filing, and, because she had no means of paying the tax or the penalties, she would be sent to jail. She hadn't kept records for her business, and the details were impossible to reconstruct. We were able attain an amnesty settlement on the basis of an indirect determination of her income and tax being paid only on the last seven years. We also obtained a waiver of civil and criminal penalties, and a reduction of interest on some of the years. Muriel was spared the ignominy of a criminal conviction and a jail sentence, and avoided financial ruin.

WHY TAXPAYERS NEED AN AMNESTY
PART II: UNREPORTED INCOME

A variety of situations can trigger a tax evader's decision to seek an amnesty.

Women Recognize the Danger First

Often the wife decides it's time for an amnesty. The husband is usually reluctant and accompanies his wife to a tax lawyer only under protest. A common tale is that taxable income has not been reported either by him alone, or by both the husband and wife. Since this evasion may have occurred over a period of several years it can add up to a significant amount of money. Men often take the position that they don't need an amnesty because they will never be caught. While it may not be explicitly stated, the person who says this obviously thinks, in his heart of hearts, that he is just too smart to be found out. There may also be some machismo involved. Women, on the other hand, just want to have the matter settled once and for all. They dread a visit from the "tax police," and the civil and possible criminal penalties that could lead to the seizure of their home, their car, their cottage, and all the other comforts money can buy.

MY NEW HUSBAND HAS NOT FILED. WHAT SHOULD I DO?

Q: *My new husband has been negligent in filing his taxes for a few years. I think it might be more than "a few years," but I'll leave it for now.*

What steps can I, as his new wife, take for filing our first "married" taxes together this year? Am I now responsible for any and/or all of his tax arrears because I married him? What steps can I start to take to be getting him back on the proper tax filing track? Any suggestions for the blindsided and burdened bride?

A: As the new bride, you are not responsible for your husband's tax debt unless he transfers assets to you. At that point, Section 160 of the Income Tax Act could kick in and make you liable for his taxes up to the amount of equity in real property, cash, investments, etc., that he transferred to you. Be vigilant and do not consent to the transfer of any assets. It would be wise to have him apply for tax amnesty before the CRA catches him and prosecutes.

It's Too Late to Pick Up the Pieces

In one instance, a wife had been urging her husband to seek our help for so long that he finally, without telling her, went to his accountant and filed all the tax returns in arrears. When the Agency reviewed the tax returns, they started to question many of the items. The questions weren't at all pretty. It seems that some unusual items were discovered, and the husband was at serious risk of criminal investigation. The wife discovered this and literally dragged her husband in to see us. Unfortunately, by filing the returns, the husband and the accountant had already put the Agency in possession of key information. There was nothing we, as lawyers, could do to mitigate the situation. We advised the taxpayer to be prepared to hire a criminal lawyer in the event he was criminally charged. We also warned him that his lawyer would be in the unfortunate position of trying to refute evidence already in the Crown's possession. The ability to protect him from criminal prosecution—along with any strategic advantage to negotiate with the Agency—had been lost.

Net-Worth or Lifestyle Assessments

Many tax evaders don't realize the danger of "living large" while reporting a modest taxable income. A very quick background check will reveal that their reported taxable income would never support their grand lifestyles. As tax lawyers, we advise these tax evaders to seek an amnesty to pre-empt a lifestyle or net-worth assessment by the Agency. After a net-worth assessment, the burden of proof to refute the Agency's findings rests entirely with the taxpayer. This is an arduous procedure and sometimes it is impossible to succeed, even in the courts.

The Angry Ex-Spouse: Your Greatest Tax Enemy

Today, successful businesswomen often earn a great deal more than their spouses do. When all is going well in the relationship, the happy couple often shares personal and financial secrets. If, at some point, things go badly, love can quickly turn to hate. More than just verbal knives come out when property has to be divided due to separation or divorce.

Here's an example from our files that shows just how far bad feelings can go after a divorce.

Cynthia was a prosperous businesswoman, married with no children. Over the past four years, she had earned very large commissions but not reported them on her tax returns. Then her marriage went on the rocks. Armed with knowledge of her tax evasion, Cynthia's soon-to-be-ex maliciously threatened to report her to the Agency. That's when she came to see us. The amount of her tax evasion was large—so large that we advised her that a criminal prosecution was almost a given. Upon conviction, she would face criminal and civil penalties, plus payment of the tax itself, plus accrued daily interest. The result would be personal and financial ruin. To say the least, this threat caused her a great deal of anxiety.

Cynthia asked us to negotiate an amnesty on her behalf. After many meetings with tax officials, we were able to reach a good settlement that included a written commitment that there would be no criminal prosecution, no civil penalties, and a reduction of interest on a portion of the outstanding amount of taxes.

We were just in the nick of time! A few days after the deal was finalized,

Cynthia's ex-husband made good on his threat and telephoned the Agency's snitch line to tell them about her tax evasion. Fortunately he was too late, and Cynthia was able to walk away unscathed from what otherwise would have been a financial and personal disaster.

Seniors: The Inadvertent Tax Evaders

When seniors realize that small tax delinquencies can put their heirs and their estate at risk, they are eager to set the record straight.

In one such case, an elderly gentleman in diminished health retained us. He had, for some sixteen years, been in receipt of a pension from another country. The pension income was not large, but it had never been declared on his tax returns in Canada. The client didn't want to be caught and penalized at his advanced stage of life. What finally pushed him to act was a family discussion. He didn't want to burden his children with his tax problems if anything happened to him. He was anxious to put his affairs in order now.

We were entrusted with negotiating an amnesty settlement on his behalf. After discussions, a written agreement was reached whereby the tax authorities confirmed that it would tax only five of the 16 years of unreported pension income. No penalties would be applied and there would be a reduction of interest in the first two years of the taxable period.

Undeclared Rental Income

In this case, our client's father had died and left her a residential property, which she rented out for 19 years without reporting the income. Now she had an offer of purchase on the house, and she knew that, as an income property, it would be subject to capital gains tax.

Suddenly, the unreported rental income became an issue. If she sold the house, the Agency would ask how she had acquired the property in the first place, and how she had used it. We successfully negotiated a settlement for our client to pay tax on eight years of rental earnings, with no civil or criminal penalties, and a reduction of interest on the tax payable of 4% in the first two years of the period. The client was now free to sell her property with a clear conscience.

In a separate case, non-residents who owned rental property in Canada had failed to report that income for many years. They wanted to sell the property, and knew that questions would be asked. In order to avoid the large penalties that would have been levied for non-reporting and tax evasion, we negotiated a settlement, which waived all penalties. Our clients were relieved to be able to declare the income and pay the tax owed without the added burden of penalties, or the threat of prosecution.

Amnesty for Offshore Trusts

The amnesty program is especially important for Canadian-resident beneficiaries of offshore trusts. Governments of all countries have become much more inquisitive and aggressive given the worldwide increase in terrorist activity. The US Government has been tapping the SWIFT database since 9/11 to trace links between suspected or known terrorist financiers and the terrorists they are funding. Since offshore tax jurisdictions are logical choices for terrorists to hide money in, officials are now very insistent on knowing just what is going on in those jurisdictions. This new tax militancy has blown a rather large hole in the claims of secrecy, which have long been put forward by tax havens.

Sabre-rattling by British, Canadian, and American tax collectors against financial advisers, and expanding exchange-of-information agreements, are making some offshore investors worried, especially those who have bent or broken Canada's tax laws. One nightmare scenario is to have the IRS pass damaging information over to the CRA's International Tax group in Ottawa. If this occurs, the result will likely be a visit by criminal enforcement officials, followed by prosecution for tax evasion and severe civil penalties. Financial ruin and jail time could easily be the result.

 The new tax militancy has blown a rather large hole in the claims of secrecy, which have long been put forward by tax havens.

Banks and other financial institutions, including international branches of large Canadian accounting firms, that have comfortably administered non-resident trusts, corporations, and investments for many years, are now looking over their collective shoulders. The off-shore arms of Canadian banks are nervous, not only about American and British questioning, but also because Canada has put new tax rules into place, which deem non-resident trusts established by a Canadian, or with a Canadian contributor or beneficiary, to be taxable in Canada.

Stringent Canadian foreign reporting requirements also require the disclosure of foreign assets, including investments, bank accounts, and interests in offshore trusts. Non-compliance will result in severe penalties, possibly including confiscation of all the assets of the offshore trust or investment. To make matters worse, there is no grandfather clause protecting the status of older trusts from the new reporting requirements.

The tax trap is quite wide, since the term "contribution" in the tax legislation includes not only a transfer, but also a loan to the trust. As the final *coup de grâce*, all parties to a trust will be jointly and individually liable for any taxes that may become due.

Not all tax haven trusts have been structured to be compliant with Canadian tax laws or international tax treaties with other jurisdictions. A review of your trust structure by an experienced tax lawyer will either set your mind at rest, or identify the need for an immediate amnesty application. Either way, it pays to know that you will be able to bring your money home safely for you or your heirs.

Here's a case from our files in which we were able to help our client declare undeclared offshore income.

Twenty-two years ago, Amanda's Aunt Minnie died in the UK, leaving Amanda what was, at that time, a relatively modest sum of money. Amanda decided to create a trust in an offshore tax haven so she could invest the money tax-free. She and her husband Richard, and their three children, all Canadian residents, were the trust's beneficiaries. Over the years, the income earned in the trust and distributed by it to the beneficiaries was never reported, even though the money was fully taxable in Canada. Now, Amanda was in her sixties, and her grown children were raising questions about how to deal with this undeclared income when it became part of their inheritance.

We discussed the alternatives with Amanda and Richard. They could keep things as they were and continue taking a chance, or they could give cash gifts to their children during their lifetime and hope that they, in turn, would not be caught by the Agency if asked about the source of the funds. The benefit of negotiating an amnesty settlement was also discussed. Amanda was most comfortable with the amnesty route. After lengthy discussions, and given a few mitigating circumstances, we were able to negotiate an arrangement with the Agency to pay tax on the earnings from the trust for only the last seven years. There would be no criminal prosecution or civil penalties, and the first two years' interest would be reduced.

Amanda and Richard now were able to bring the money legally into Canada, to be used by them, or distributed to their children, as they saw fit.

WHEN AMNESTY GOES AWRY

The cases we have shared from our tax law practice files make the amnesty process appear easy and straightforward. Nothing could be further from the truth.

As experienced tax lawyers, we have acquired unique insight and understanding of the tax laws and the Agency's mindset. Remember, in our tax law practice, we handle only cases that involve resolving taxpayer problems with the Agency.

When we start work on a taxpayer's behalf, we already have a decided strategic advantage. Without that advantage, without experienced legal counsel and the confidentiality of lawyer-client privilege, an amnesty negotiation can go very wrong, exposing the taxpayer to the full brunt of the law.

The most important fact to remember in any negotiation with the Agency is that CRA agents are not bound by what they "tell" you. To be binding, any agreement with them must be in writing. To be legally binding, a lawyer-negotiated settlement in writing is essential. Do-it-yourself aficionados run a real risk in trying to negotiate their own amnesty.

Here are some examples of what can go wrong:

Example 1

A senior disclosed to tax authorities that he had not reported an offshore pension income that he had been receiving for the past 21 years. When he discovered that this failure to report had turned him unwittingly into a tax evader, he approached the Agency on his own to negotiate an amnesty. He met with a CRA agent who was quite understanding and agreed that they should able to clear this up easily. They agreed verbally that the senior would pay the tax owing on a small portion of the 21 years of unreported pension income, and the senior believed the deal was done. Then the Agency's reassessment arrived in the mail.

The poor man almost had a heart attack on the spot. He was assessed back taxes on the full 21 years of pension income, with daily accrued interest. It added up to a tremendous sum—so large that he was financially ruined. There was nothing this senior could do. He had made the mistake of trusting a verbal deal with the Agency.

An amnesty settlement is, at all times, a discretionary decision made by the Agency. It has the authority to offer reduced interest and penalties, and even to waive the tax owing for some of the years disclosed. But it is never obliged to do so. And, once an amnesty decision is made, it cannot be changed—even by the CRA's head office committee in charge of taxpayer relief provisions.

The senior thought he could save money by not hiring a tax lawyer to represent him. In retrospect, his decision was "penny wise, pound foolish." In our hands, his case would have been presented to the Agency on a no-name basis, with no disclosure of his name or identifying details, until a favourable settlement had been agreed to in writing. Because of the man's advanced age, there may have been mitigating circumstances, such as ill health or an inability to pay that could have aided our negotiations. We might also have secured a waiver or reduction of interest for some of the tax years involved. Had the Agency declined to consider these factors, the elderly gentleman could have walked away from the amnesty application without the Agency knowing his name. It is our practice not to leave the bargaining table until a good settlement is reached for our client. There is little doubt that we could have spared this gentleman from the devastating outcome his unaided efforts produced.

Example 2

Another recent case, reported in the *Globe and Mail*, April 27, 2006, illustrates how a private individual tried to negotiate his own amnesty and shot himself in the foot instead. Here's a recap of the situation, taken from news reports.

The tax evader was in a messy divorce dispute and, in a desperate attempt to divert funds from his ex-wife, decided to tell the tax department about the tax returns he hadn't filed for nine years. He wanted to come clean and make an amnesty deal. He would pay the tax he owed with some interest, provided the Agency agreed to absolve him and not prosecute him for the tax evasion. The Agency would get some serious money out of him. More importantly, his wife would be prevented from claiming that money in her divorce suit.

According to the article, the tax evader's lawyer advised against the strategy. It was too dangerous, he said. Better to battle out the divorce settlement and not let the Agency know about the unfiled tax returns. But the tax evader was convinced he knew better; he sat down with the Agency on his own to negotiate an amnesty. In short order, a deal was negotiated and the tax evader was to be granted an amnesty pending filing of the outstanding tax returns. The returns were filed. Then, the Agency started digging into the facts, something that happens often. It turned out that the tax evader hadn't made a complete disclosure in his amnesty application and the Agency had an opening to repudiate the amnesty. Now the Agency wanted nearly $2 million in taxes, penalties, and interest, and prosecution had not been ruled out. The tax evader was furious and took the Agency to court, claiming entrapment. He lost his case. The judge ruled that his lawyer had given him good advice not to come forward to the Agency at that particular time, but he had ignored it. Entrapment didn't apply.

We can only hope this tax evader has a good criminal lawyer to keep him out of jail should criminal charges be filed.

10

SURVIVING A TAX AUDIT

The purpose of every tax audit is to increase your tax
owing, add penalties and interest, and, if
possible, build a case for criminal investigation.

—Former CRA Audit Review Supervisor

Deep down in our heart of hearts we are all afraid that, one day, the
Agency will come to call at our homes or places of business. We should
be afraid. A tax audit is never a good thing. Few come through it
unscathed. The process of answering a challenge to every financial
and accounting decision made over the period of time in question will
exact a huge emotional toll from even the most stout-hearted and honest taxpayer. And, if we expect to be rewarded for not taking certain
deductions we might have claimed, but didn't, think again.

In the words of one former CRA Audit Review Supervisor, "I
have never seen the outcome of an audit assessment in the taxpayer's
favour."

This is not to say it can never happen. But if, in the course of dec-
ades of service in the tax department, such a senior supervisor never

saw an audit settled in favour of the taxpayer, one has to assume that the odds of coming out on top of the Agency are very, very slim.

Of all the interactions a taxpayer may have with the Agency, the audit is one of the most dangerous. Why? The purpose of every audit is to gather evidence to increase your taxes, add penalties and interest, and, if warranted, recommend to the Justice Department that you be criminally prosecuted for tax evasion.

A tax auditor is trained to apply the most rigorous interpretation of the Income Tax Act to his investigation of a taxpayer's accounts. Under such microscopic examination, it is almost inevitable the audit will uncover discrepancies in accounting practices, or simple reporting errors, or any of a number of anomalies that the Agency will interpret as deliberate attempts to mislead the tax authorities and cheat the CRA out of its not-so-fair share of your money. These errors or discrepancies will allow the Agency to assess additional tax in the year or years audited, along with penalties and daily interest on both the newly assessed tax owing and the penalties. Most damaging of all, the interest will be calculated daily from the due date of the tax return for that year, or years. Where misrepresentation, error, or fraud can be shown, it doesn't matter if it occurred 5, 10, or even 20 years in the past. In such a situation there is no time limit.

The purpose of every audit is to gather evidence to increase your taxes, add penalties and interest, and, if warranted, recommend to the Justice Department that you be criminally prosecuted for tax evasion.

On this basis, even a modest reassessment can mushroom into a tax debt so huge that, even if you sold your home and your car, and liquidated all your other assets, you still would not have enough money to pay the Agency. The financial burden may be just the start of the nightmare if you are also charged with tax evasion and have to face the Agency in criminal court. It's easy to understand why the tax audit is the Agency's most profitable endeavour.

Later in this section we will look at how the Agency decides who to audit, what it looks for during an audit, and how it will try to entrap you into exposing your tax-related financial shortcomings so that it can recover as much revenue as possible. You'll also find a crucial list of do's and don'ts if you ever are selected for an audit.

TAX AUDIT 101: BASIC DEFINITIONS

What Is an Audit?

An audit is an examination of your financial accounts. It is a way to ascertain the correctness of your tax returns. According to the Canadian Institute of Chartered Accountants, the purpose of an audit of financial statements is to be able to express an opinion about whether or not they present fairly the financial position, results of operations, and changes in financial position of the party being audited. Of course, this must all be done in accordance with generally accepted accounting principles. A tax audit uses this process to assess your level of tax compliance. As stated earlier, its purpose is to increase your taxes, assess civil penalties, and, if possible, build a case for criminal investigation. It's not something to trivialize.

Why Are Audits Performed?

Our tax system makes taxpayers individually responsible for calculating their tax payable for each taxation year based on guidelines provided by the CRA. Each taxpayer is also responsible for filing a return every year, and then remitting the amount due. Each business must also file a return and forward payment. The law puts the onus on the filing taxpayer to prove, if demanded, all claims made in the return. Since you signed the return, certifying it to be correct, you usually cannot blame your accountant for any errors or discrepancies.

It is assumed that a certain percentage of taxpayers will take advantage of this self-reporting system by not filing tax returns, or not fully and honestly disclosing all their sources of income. Therefore, provisions are built into the tax act Income Tax Act mandating the keeping of books and records so that the Agency can, at will, demand to review the taxpayer's accounts to determine tax liability.

What Powers Does the Agency Have?

Some of the Agency's powers to investigate are outlined in Section 231.1(1) of the Income Tax Act (2007). To read the full provisions of this and other relevant sections, consult *CCH Income Tax Act 2007*. The scope of these provisions is staggering, and everyone should know their extent. To summarize,

An authorized person may:

(a) inspect, audit, or examine the books and records of a taxpayer and any document of the taxpayer or of any other person that relates or may relate to the information that is or should be in the books or records of the taxpayer or to any amount payable by him under this Act, and

(b) examine the property of a taxpayer or matter relating to the taxpayer or any other person, an examination of which may assist in determining the accuracy of the inventory (property) of the taxpayer or in ascertaining the information that is or should be in the books or records of the taxpayer or any amount payable by him under the Income Tax Act.

2,600

The number of individuals prosecuted for failing to file a tax return in the 2004–2005 fiscal year.

Section 231 also permits the Agency to demand at will any information or document. (See "Formal Requirement for Information," in Chapter 7.) Failure to produce the requested material can have serious consequences, including prosecution for criminal tax evasion.

In addition to the right to audit the taxpayer, the Income Tax Act also gives the Agency the power to recommend that the Department of Justice criminally prosecute evaders for failure to file a tax return, and failure to fully and openly disclose all income from all sources on a tax return.

> *Section 238(1):* Every person who has failed to file a return as and when required by or under this Act . . . is guilty of an offence and in addition to any penalty otherwise provided is liable on summary conviction to a fine of not less than $1,000 and imprisonment for a term not exceeding 12 months.
>
> *Section 239(1):* Every person who has made false or deceptive statements in a return to evade payment of tax . . . is liable on summary conviction to a fine of not less than 50% . . . and up to 200% and imprisonment for a term not exceeding two years.

This means that an audit can turn into a criminal investigation at the stroke of a bureaucratic pen. All the information uncovered in the course of the audit is admissible in court as evidence against you. By cooperating with the Agency, you effectively hand it the evidence for the case against you.

Your only protection is to preserve your ability to invoke your Charter rights against self-incrimination during the audit on the assumption that it will turn into a criminal investigation.

 An audit can turn into a criminal investigation at the stroke of a bureaucratic pen.

YOUR LEGAL RIGHTS

Sections 7 and 8 of the Charter of Rights and Freedoms state:

> *Section 7.* Everyone has the right to life, liberty, and security of the person and the right not to be deprived thereof except in accordance with the principles of fundamental justice.
>
> *Section 8.* Everyone has the right to be secure against unreasonable search and seizure.

The right to remain silent applies during the investigative stage if the Agency is investigating criminal behaviour.

The problem is: How do you know if the Agency is simply reviewing your information to make an accurate assessment of taxes, or if it is reviewing your information as a means to gather evidence to be used in a criminal investigation? Until you are informed that you are the subject of a criminal investigation, or until you are formally charged, you won't know. Often, during the course of an audit, there is an overlap between the civil investigation and the criminal investigation. Yet, your Charter right to remain silent is not triggered until such time as you are under criminal investigation. It presents the taxpayer with a difficult dilemma.

As a taxpayer and a citizen, your best course of action is to set up a legal firewall as soon as you receive a Notice of Audit. An experienced tax lawyer will cooperate with the Agency while the audit is still only an audit, providing only what is specifically requested and/or relevant to the specific tax years and file under audit. Thus, if the audit should become a criminal investigation, you have a better chance of invoking your Charter rights, which can help to protect you from self-incrimination.

TYPES OF AUDITS

Following is a description of the three principal types of audit: correspondence audits, office audits, and field audits. For more detailed information on how to handle an audit properly, see "Coping with an Audit" later in this chapter.

Correspondence Audits

A correspondence audit is the simplest of the audit processes. The Agency will send a written notice that you or your business has been selected for review with the request that you provide specific information and/or records. The presumption is that the Agency will review what you send on its own time and terms, and then follow up as it deems necessary. If no serious discrepancies or anomalies are found in your records, this type of assessment may conclude with a simple reassessment for more tax, penalties, and interest owing. Or it may escalate and turn into an office audit or a field audit.

Office Audits

An office audit usually takes place at the local tax services office. The Agency will send a written notice to you specifying the date, time, and place of the audit, and the documents that you are required to bring along. This type of audit means the Agency has some concerns that it wishes to review with you in person. If you decide to attend, be very careful what you say. It can and will be used against you.

Field Audits

A field audit usually takes place at the taxpayer's home or place of business. The Agency will send a written notice that you or your business has been selected for review. Normally, it sets out the period that is under review and what information must be provided. The field auditor has a great deal of discretion in determining what items are to be reviewed and the scope of the audit.

As part of a field audit, the tax official may ask for a tour of your business premises. This proposed tour is part of a plan to try to get information as to how well the business is doing. Even if no immediate notes appear to be taken, his or her observations will be filed away mentally. Anything the auditor sees or hears will be construed as a voluntary disclosure of information. Their position is, if you didn't want the auditor to see what was happening in your business, you wouldn't have taken him or her on the tour. In effect, by agreeing to the tour, you can be construed to have waived your Charter right against self-incrimination. The information gained can, therefore, be used against you as evidence in a criminal tax evasion prosecution.

Do you have to agree to take the auditor on the tour? NO. You may and should decline to do so. Of course, this could make the auditor think you have something to hide. Since the purpose of the audit is to prove this anyway, you are better off protecting your privacy at this stage of the process.

WHY ME? HOW DOES THE AGENCY DECIDE WHOM TO AUDIT?

There are a number of ways to be selected for an audit.

Random Selection

This is simply the luck of the draw. Every year, a certain number of taxpayer files are randomly selected for audit. If your name comes up, you get an audit letter. There's nothing you can do to prevent yourself from being selected for an audit in this manner. You can, however, protect yourself and keep the audit from turning into a nightmare. We will discuss this in more detail later in this chapter.

Statistical Anomalies

The Agency uses statistics to set normal ratios of revenue to expenses for each industry. The calculations are based upon Statistics Canada data on the costs of doing business in specific business areas, cross-referenced to the cost of carrying on that type of business in various locations of the country. If the ratio of revenue to expenses on your tax return significantly differs from the Agency's benchmark, your file very likely will be red-flagged for audit. Certain industries are known to be more prone to audit, in part because tax filers in those industries frequently trigger the red flag. Self-employed small-business owners often attract the attention of the Agency in this manner.

The CRA's matching program also plays a role in determining which taxpayer files will be audited. (See Chapter 3.)

Unusual or Suspicious Behaviour

This refers to any sudden or obvious change in your tax filing behaviour. For instance, if you have been filing tax returns for many years and then suddenly stop, the Agency will wonder what happened to you. It may let you continue unchallenged for a few years before requesting an audit of your books and records. This allows the Agency to collect more penalties and interest when they do come after you. But make no mistake, the Agency will seek you out eventually.

Another common scenario is that of the non-filer who suddenly starts filing tax returns with no apparent history of tax filing. People do this for several reasons. Guilt over tax evasion—or a spouse's fear of being caught—may prompt a tax delinquent to finally come clean. Or perhaps the evader has taken a salaried job after years of cash-under-the-table self-employment, immediately exposing him or her to Agency scrutiny. Or perhaps a taxpayer needs to produce tax returns to qualify for a loan or mortgage, or needs to file in order to collect Canada Pension Plan payments. Whatever the reason, if the Agency senses unusual behaviour, it will investigate, and an audit notice may arrive in the mail. Those who have this type of problem should read the chapter on lawyer-negotiated settlements (Chapter 9) and cover themselves by obtaining a settlement with the Agency before filing any tax returns.

Somebody Snitched

Don't think this could never happen to you! A neighbour, an ex-spouse, a business competitor, a creditor, someone you think of as a friend—anyone can choose to make an anonymous call to the Agency's snitch line. If the Agency can't find you in its records, or if the situation appears suspicious, you suddenly will become of great interest and very likely get an invitation to an audit.

When Am I Safe from a Reassessment or Audit?

Normally, in the absence of significant taxpayer error, misrepresentation, or fraud, the Agency's clock stops running three years after the mailing date on your Notice of Assessment for each taxation year. An exception to this general rule is when a tax shelter is involved. However, the caveat is that, in all but the simplest situations, you may never really be safe. If inappropriate business expenses have been claimed, more than minor mathematical errors made, or some taxable revenue not reported, the Agency could choose to audit and reassess you at any time, on the basis of misrepresentation.

COPING WITH AN AUDIT—CRUCIAL DO'S AND DON'TS

The secret to dealing with any audit request, whatever the type, is to maintain proper records. Unfortunately, most of us are not, by nature, good bookkeepers. (Those who are become accountants or tax officials.) Without reasonably good records, you're just looking for serious trouble when you head into an audit. If you aren't able to document your claims clearly, it will be all too easy for the Agency to assess additional tax. It doesn't end there. The Agency has many penalties it can also apply and there will be daily interest on the tax and the penalties. If your records are poor, you might not be able to do much about it now. But at least you can go into an audit with your eyes open. The "nice" people at the tax agency are not your friends, even though they will call you their "client." They have their own agenda—it's to empty your pockets to the greatest extent legally possible.

When selected for an office audit, you will be expected to attend a meeting at your local tax services office with all the records that were requested. If you can't gather these records and the documents needed to substantiate the items questioned by the Agency, you can ask for a postponement. It's best to do this in writing, but a telephone call followed by written confirmation is also acceptable. If the postponement is granted and you still cannot obtain all the required documents, request another postponement. If this is not granted, then attend the audit with whatever records you have and inform the auditor, in person, that you need more time to secure the remaining documents, and outline the reasons that make a postponement necessary.

During the office audit, you can count on having to verify total business income, and expenses such as payments to subcontractors, travel and entertainment expenses, automobile expenses, major purchases, and any other expense that appears to be large in relation to your total business income. The auditor can examine each and every expense for the entire period under review, or may choose to select a month or two on a sample basis. An office audit can be routine, if your records are in good order and your tax reporting is, to the best of your knowledge, completely truthful and accurate. In this scenario, your audit may be resolved fairly smoothly. But be prepared for an increased tax assessment. Remember, you are a CRA profit centre.

If you are selected for a field audit, the procedure will be much more in-depth and invasive. Consider doing everything in your power to request that you meet with the Agency on neutral ground. This would entail retaining an advocate—a tax lawyer or tax professional working under the protection of a tax lawyer—to be with you when you meet with the Agency, so that you can request to meet at your advocate's offices. This strategy can keep the Agency from snooping around your home or business.

The Field Auditor's Sheet

When the field auditor does pay a visit to a taxpayer's home or business, he or she has a specific agenda of discovery. The questions the auditor will try to ask you are frankly horrifying in terms of how they invade your personal financial privacy. Below are two of the more frightening questions. To view a detailed re-creation of the field auditor's form, visit our website at *www.taxrx.ca/auditorsforms*.

a) Personal bank accounts:
What are all the personal bank accounts, types, and locations for the period under audit and the current year?

b) Spouse's personal bank accounts:
Nature and source of deposits to spouse's personal accounts? (drawings/wages/sale of personal assets)

Any non-taxable sources of funds? (inheritances/lottery winnings/gifts/gambling)

Have you lent or given money personally? (to family, friends, etc.)

List real property bought, sold, or owned currently and during the audit period.
Principal/Primary Residence
Cottages/Time Shares/Vacation Properties

List vehicles bought, sold, or owned during the audit period. (automobiles; boats/yachts/planes; motorbikes/all-terrain vehicles; recreation vehicles/trailers)

Any individual or family vacations taken during the audit period? (obtain details)

c) Children's bank accounts:
Number and ages of children:
Financial Institution, Acct. Numbers, Type of Account, Signing Authority

What is the nature and source of deposits to children's personal accounts and nature and purpose of any withdrawals?

If you are ever presented with a form like this, *do not under any circumstances begin to answer any of these questions.* Politely decline and say instead that your legal counsel will work with the Agency auditor to provide any necessary details.

The Value of an Advocate

There are other reasons to work with an advocate. Even before it meets with you, the Agency assumes you are guilty. The burden of proof to prove your innocence is always on you, the taxpayer. You really don't want to deal directly with the auditor working on your case. You may become confused, and the auditor is trained to try to get you to volunteer information not directly related to the items in question or taxation years involved in the audit.

"Lovely children," the auditor might say, noting the silver-framed photos of your progeny on your desk. "And do they all go to private schools?" Or, "Is this your family cottage? It looks like Muskoka. And what a nice boat."

You really don't want the auditor to see where you live or work.

Tax auditors are trained to collect any information that could be used to increase your taxable income, or to disallow some expenses you thought were deductible. After all, they want to use such information to build a case against you. They need to fish for information.

Your best protection is to retain a qualified advocate with a good deal of experience in tax law to stand between you and the auditor at every stage of your audit journey.

Before hiring a tax advocate, get full details of his or her training and experience. You don't want your advocate learning how to do his or her job on your time and perhaps fouling up your defence to the proposed audit. Next, do a due diligence and check out the references. Does he or she have professional credentials? Has he or she successfully represented others in an audit? Is he or she considered trustworthy? This is no time to practice so-called grey accounting.

AUDIT RULES TO LIVE BY

- **Don't panic.** You don't have to stand alone in front of the CRA auditor. You are entitled to engage a qualified representative (tax lawyer, tax professional, etc.) to go in your place. Remember, the Agency is trying to take as much of your money as is legally possible, so don't be shy about exercising your right to counsel.

- **Only one spokesperson deals with the auditor.** This avoids contradictory answers that may be used to incriminate you later.

- **Request the auditor's questions in advance.** Get them in writing and answer them in writing before you meet.

- **Don't justify.** Normally at the initial stage of an audit, it is not necessary or even beneficial for you to try to justify your position. It may just give the auditor ideas and lead to matters that are otherwise not on the radar screen.

- **Manage your files carefully.** Don't automatically hand over sensitive or privileged information. The auditor may not need to see it. Moreover, when files are handed over, you have waived your privilege of confidentiality and may have voluntarily provided the Agency with evidence of wrongdoing. Once waived, that privilege cannot be re-established, even if you hire legal counsel at a later stage of the audit. This is just one reason why it is important to have an experienced tax lawyer assist you from the beginning of the audit.

- **Don't try to pull a fast one.** Playing games by trying to transfer the title of the family home is a favourite ploy among those facing an unpleasant situation with the Agency. If you get an audit letter, it's too late to put the house in your spouse's name. It won't protect your home and, even worse, it will involve your spouse in your tax problems. The same holds true for your other assets. Trying to transfer assets in a hurry tells the Agency in no uncertain terms that you really do have something to hide. It will respond by digging deeper into your affairs.

- **Thoroughly brief your advocate.** Discuss the matter with your own representative to ensure the issues are determined before meeting with the auditor.

- **Don't talk to the auditor yourself.** We can't stress this enough! Don't respond to the auditor's telephone request for additional information yourself. Have your representative deal with it in writing.

- **Don't be forced into a meeting.** A favourite CRA ploy is to demand an immediate meeting. Postpone such a meeting until your advocate is properly prepared to deal with the situation. If the Agency threatens or harasses you into agreeing to a meeting, have your advocate bring a tape recorder to the meeting, and then ask for time to respond in writing.

- **Don't just roll over.** Some taxpayers just want to get the audit over with and will make admissions simply to get the Agency to go away. In our experience, this serves to whet the appetite of the tax beast. Stand up to the Agency unless your advocate recommends that a settlement is in your best interest.

HOW TO REDUCE YOUR CHANCES OF AN AUDIT

There is an old saying that "an ounce of prevention is worth a pound of cure." While there is no foolproof way to avoid becoming the target of a tax audit, there are ways to reduce your risk of being audited.

- **File your tax returns on time.** Don't wait until the Agency sends a request or Demand to File. As a non-filer for more than one year if tax is due you will have to pay civil penalties and interest for late filing in addition to having to pay your taxes. You may be criminally prosecuted, to boot.

- **Check your return.** Check the math. Make sure you included all required information: name, address, social insurance number, marital status, and so on. Don't forget to sign your return. Remember, your signature is a legally-binding statement that your return is complete and truthful.

- **Keep good records.** The law places the burden of proof on you to prove your innocence to the Agency. To do that, you need proper documentation. If that's a problem, don't give up. If you are audited and lack the information to support your case, an experienced tax lawyer working in tandem with a good accountant should be able to help you overcome the problem.

- **Report all your income.** If you are a salaried employee, the Agency has copies of all your T4 slips and matches them with what you report. If they discover a discrepancy, they will eventually ask you to amend your return, and then levy a fine. Depending on the magnitude of your under-reporting and the period of time involved, the Agency may also choose to prosecute you for evasion.

Think you can hide your money in a foreign country? As discussed earlier, Canada has information-sharing agreements with tax authorities in other countries. If the Agency asks, foreign governments and banks will provide records of your financial transactions. Since 9/11, even tax havens can no longer boast of total financial secrecy. If you have been hiding money offshore, seek the advice of a tax lawyer *now*, before the Agency catches you.

- **Claim only legitimate business expenses.** Business expense deductions must be reasonable and legitimately incurred in the course of generating taxable revenue. Do not claim personal expenses as business deductions or over-inflate your expenses. This will make you exceed the statistical norms for your industry and could trigger an audit red flag.

- **Don't cheat.** The old saying that "cheaters never prosper" is true for those who take cash under the table for services rendered, or who conveniently forget to mention the extra weekend job. The Agency is always watching.

HOW TO INCREASE YOUR CHANCES OF SURVIVING AN AUDIT INTACT

- **Get help.** The first decision to make when you get an audit notice is whether to handle it yourself or seek help. Retaining a qualified and experienced tax advocate costs money but, in the end, saves you stress and time, and may possibly protect you from financial ruin and criminal prosecution. The "I have nothing to hide" philosophy is foolish at best and dangerous at worst.
- **Be prepared.** Review the tax returns and gather all requested documentation. If you discover an overstatement of income or understatement of expenses, your advocate should bring it to the attention of the tax auditor. If, however, you discover the reverse, discuss this with your advocate so that a decision can be made as to the most favourable way to share this information with the Agency.
- **Don't lose your cool.** If you attend the audit yourself—and we recommend you do not—keep control of your anger and resentment. At all times, maintain a correct and courteous attitude. Sometimes it is very hard, especially if the auditor is aggressive and impolite. While this is rare, it does happen. One client

told us of an audit meeting he attended before he engaged our law firm, during which the tax auditor, whose cultural background was not Canadian, told him, "In my country, what you did would put you in danger of having your head cut off." We would suggest the best response to such a provocative statement would be to smile and say nothing. However, if you must answer, say something like: "We should both be grateful that we don't do that in Canada." The bottom line is, while you may be very angry with the auditor, or with the Agency in general, ranting and raving will only make the auditor search harder for ways to assess you for more tax, interest, and penalties.

- **Don't volunteer information.** If you ignore the advice in this book and insist on talking to the auditor on your own, provide only what has been requested, and only discuss the matters in question. Don't let the Agency turn your audit into a fishing expedition for the Agency to build a better case.

- **Never smile at a crocodile.** Don't trust the "good cop" tax auditor. Unless a routine examination reveals the likelihood of unreported income, the Agency is not entitled to conduct an indirect determination of income (net worth), and cannot demand that you complete a statement of your annual estimated personal and family expenses to determine how you lived on the income reported on your return. The estimated expenses form is quite lengthy and requests information on a number of highly personal issues, including how much you spend on gifts for your grandchildren, tobacco and alcohol, flowers for the church, and even lottery tickets. You can view a sample Personal Expenditures Worksheet in its entirety on our website at *www.taxrx.ca/networthassessmentforms*. Do not complete a form such as this—or even answer such questions verbally—unless on the advice of, and with the help of, legal counsel. Everything on this form can be used against you at a later stage of your audit, or even in criminal court. If the tax auditor, with proper justification, insists that completion of the personal expenses sheet is absolutely necessary, make it clear that you will complete it with the help of your advocate. Under no circumstances let the "friendly" auditor help.

- **Don't argue with the tax auditor.** If the auditor indicates that he or she wants to disallow a deduction, or otherwise increase the tax you owe, and you don't agree, state your disagreement calmly and only once. Remember, after the audit is completed, a tax lawyer can file a Notice of Objection to the assessment on your behalf and, if this fails, take your case to the tax court.

- **Don't be intimidated.** An audit is a daunting experience, and sometimes it may feel like an inquisition. But the power of the auditor is limited. Don't automatically provide everything just because the auditor asked for it. For example, if the auditor requests access to your accountant's files and records, try to find out what the auditor specifically wishes to check that can't be found in your own records. Then make sure your accountant's files contain only source documents. Remove any memos, emails, or correspondence that could prejudice your case. Your tax lawyer should definitely be involved in overseeing this type of request.

- **Don't interfere with search and seizure.** This is an extreme situation in which the auditor has a warrant entitling him or her to seize your records. You must not interfere if you are faced with this scenario. You are, however, entitled to insist that your tax lawyer verify the validity of the search warrant after the fact. It may be possible to make a claim of privilege, at which point the documents in question must be sealed and delivered into the custody of a court official.

- **Seek legal counsel before you answer any CRA questionnaire. It could be a trap!** In *Stanfield et al vs. Minister of*

National Revenue (2005), tax agency officials sent several taxpayers letters requesting audit information relating to their large business losses from trading. The Agency believed that these taxpayers had invested in suspected tax shelters or other tax avoidance schemes set up by promoters. Field Audit had forwarded the initial audit information to the Criminal Investigations unit. Then the criminal investigation was allegedly stopped. According to the CRA, the information was transferred back to audit, which sent letters to the taxpayers asking a series of questions about their association with specific companies, promotion and advice received, representations about predetermined losses, financing, accounts outside Canada, and non-resident trusts. Throughout the questioning process, audit personnel remained in regular contact with criminal investigators. By the time these letters and questionnaires were sent, the normal reassessment period for most of the tax years in question had expired and audits had already determined reassessments. The taxpayers refused to complete the questionnaires and litigation ensued. Upon judicial review of the case, the Agency questionnaires were quashed. The Agency's actions were deemed incorrect because the predominant purpose of its questionnaires was to collect documents and information for a criminal investigation. The civil auditors were found to be effectively acting as agents for criminal investigations. The Court found the audit team could have carried out reassessments without these questionnaires. The taxpayers' Charter rights to remain silent and avoid self-incrimination were upheld.

SOME SPECIFIC THINGS THE AUDITOR MIGHT CHECK

Withholding Taxes

Payments of dividends, interest, rents, or other periodic profits to non-residents of Canada must be reported by the payor and taxes deducted. If the tax is not remitted and a report filed, the remitter may be personally responsible for paying the tax.

Foreign Property Reporting

The Income Tax Act requires reporting, with some exceptions, of foreign property owned by a taxpayer where the cost amount exceeds $100,000.

Reporting of a Foreign Trust

Generally speaking, the Income Tax Act requires reporting of any distribution of property held by a foreign trust.

Director's Liability for Unremitted Withholding Taxes

The Income Tax Act imposes personal liability on the director of a corporation with respect to the non-remission of employees' source deductions to the government. There is also personal responsibility to collect and remit the GST/HST. The Agency normally looks to the corporation to pay these amounts. But, if the corporation goes out of business and does not have the assets to pay, then the CRA will come after the directors themselves. The rules also apply to non-profit corporations and charities. If you are a director of a charity, you can be liable for its source deductions and GST/HST if the charity fails to pay them.

The Agency also assesses what it calls "de facto directors." If you act as a director or hold yourself out as a director, even though no formal appointment was made, you can be held liable.

A Notice of Assessment for director's liability must be issued within two years of the date you have ceased to be a director. Therefore, if there is any possibility you may be responsible for past actions of the corporation and have yet to be assessed, resign immediately. A Notice of Change of Directors must be filed with the provincial corporation registry. As soon as you have formally resigned, the "two-year clock" starts running. You will not be liable unless the Agency assesses the corporation and then issues you a Notice of Assessment within the two-year period.

While there can be a due diligence defence for failure to comply, it's quite difficult to escape personal liability. The success or failure of a due diligence defence can hinge on whether or not the subject corporation has a history of late GST/HST remittances. The onus of proof to establish a good due diligence defence will be on the offending director.

Being unaware of the corporation's financial situation does not relieve a director from liability. It is important that a director exercises a reasonable degree of care, diligence, and skill, and is prudent. Otherwise, he or she will personally be on the hook to pay the GST/HST or source deductions that were not remitted as required.

There are various measures that a director can take to establish a due diligence defence. These include

- establishing a bank account for withholdings from employees and remittances of source deductions, as well as for remittances of GST/HST
- having corporate financial officers report regularly on the status of the account
- obtaining regular confirmation that withholdings and remittances have, in fact, been made during all relevant periods

If you are a director of a corporation and the firm is being audited, you may wish to protect yourself by retaining your own legal counsel. Some may say this will make it look as though you have something to hide. But if the Agency comes sniffing after you, it will assume you are hiding something anyway, so it's better to be protected.

AFTER THE INTERVIEWS—YOUR PROPOSED ASSESSMENT

Once the auditor has finished asking questions and reviewing your records, you will receive a letter proposing an assessment. It is supposed to contain a summary of the facts for, an analysis of, and the authority for the proposed assessment. Your advocate should ask the CRA auditor to explain the reasoning for its assessing position.

At this point, submissions can be made to dispute adjustments proposed by the CRA. If its response to you is negative and you feel an error has been made, you can deal with the auditor's group head or, if warranted, you may try to speak to someone at a higher level in the Agency. A settlement of the issues involved might be worked out at this point, possibly bypassing the objection and appeal process altogether.

 Even if you are disputing the outcome of your audit through the proper legal channels, the Agency can still file a lien against your house or other property.

AFTER THE AUDIT——ASSESSMENT AND COLLECTION

Once the audit is finalized and a summary of the findings has been mailed to you, you will receive a Notice of Assessment. Unless you have already filed a Notice of Objection, the amount due is payable immediately. Any remaining unpaid tax debt can be certified by the Agency and registered in the federal court. This has the same force and effect as a judgment of that court. The fact that a taxpayer has filed a Notice of Objection to the assessment doesn't affect the Agency's right to certify the debt and register the certificate. Thus, even if you are disputing the outcome of your audit through the proper legal channels, the Agency can still file a lien against your house or other property. Other collection procedures are normally stayed or reduced until the ruling is made on your objection.

Keep in mind while you are moving through the legal channels in your dispute with the Agency that daily interest on the tax and penalties is accumulating. The longer your dispute drags on, the more astronomical the total of your tax debt. As tax lawyers, we recommend that you don't wait to pay the tax assessed—even if the chances of winning your objection are very good. Paying "under protest" is the only way to protect yourself from the relentless accumulation of daily interest. If you are successful in your objection, the Agency will be required to repay you what it owes with interest. The rub is that this interest must be declared as part of your taxable income in the coming tax year.

What the Agency gives with one hand, it usually finds a way to take back with the other. Some things never change.

A TALE OF TWO TAX AUDITS

The Case of the Delinquent Mover

This case from our files demonstrates that, even on the brink of ruin, there is salvation.

Charlie owned and operated a moving business. He started out small with one truck—then a second truck was acquired. Then Charlie decided to buy more vehicles to meet the demands of a larger customer base. But after what looked liked a promising start, Charlie discovered he wasn't generating enough revenue to pay the monthly bills and wages of his drivers and helpers.

He talked to his bank. It wanted the family home assigned as collateral security for a loan. The home was registered in his wife Anne's name—a wise tax-planning strategy, they had thought—and she was unhappy with the prospect of encumbering the home. It was their only clear asset and the family nest where they were raising their two children. So Charlie and Anne turned down the bank's demand and the bank, in turn, refused Charlie's request for a loan.

Things went from bad to worse. Because money was tight, Charlie hadn't been filing income tax or GST returns, and had failed to remit source deductions for his employees. Charlie didn't think he'd get caught because the business had never been registered. He thought he was off the Agency's radar. And for a while, he was right. For several years nobody came after him. What Charlie didn't fully appreciate was that while he remained undetected, the taxes on his unreported income plus unremitted GST, and the unpaid source deductions for his employees kept accumulating. Interest and penalties were also accruing daily.

He might have continued to escape detection for years. But one day a jealous competitor decided to call the Agency's anonymous snitch line, just to "make sure" Charlie was paying his fair share of taxes. The Agency, which had no record of Charlie's business, was suddenly very interested and asked for details. The snitch was only too happy to oblige. Shortly thereafter a letter from the CRA arrived with a request that Charlie file his tax returns along with a notice that the Agency would be coming to audit the books and records of his business.

Charlie and Anne were distraught. Charlie knew he had been playing a dangerous game. Now the jig was up and the financial cost would be high. Fortunately, he also knew it was time to seek serious help and called us.

At the first meeting, Charlie and Anne had the stricken look of deer caught in the headlights. Our initial estimate was that the total GST, source deductions, and unreported income tax owed, including interest and penalties, added up to nearly $200,000. It was an amount Charlie and Anne never could pay. We suggested it might be possible to negotiate a reduction or waiver of penalties and interest through a negotiated equity settlement with the Agency.

Charlie thought it would be easier for him to declare bankruptcy and start a new business. He had done this before when he had owed the Agency a lot of money and, according to him, "it had worked like a charm."

But dealing with the Agency is never that simple. A second bankruptcy application at this stage could trigger a review of Charlie's first bankruptcy and possibly reopen the tax files on that defunct business. If the Agency didn't like what it found, Charlie could be hauled into criminal court on charges of tax evasion. A conviction would leave him with a criminal record and a fine of up to 200% of the tax, plus interest. Failure to pay this fine would mean a jail term. At the same time, the Agency could challenge the second bankruptcy and try to prevent him from receiving a discharge.

Anne had her own set of worries. Charlie's business supported Anne and their two children—one of whom was quite ill and required constant attention—as well as Charlie's aged and ailing parents. This personal stress, plus the problems with the business, had already taken a huge toll on the couple; both had been under doctor's treatment for the last year and a half.

Tax lawyers do not have magic answers to everyone's tax problems. But in many circumstances, it is possible to help clients avoid criminal and civil penalties and negotiate a reasonable settlement. We believed Charlie's case could be resolved this way if handled properly. Charlie agreed to retain us as legal counsel.

The plan to save Charlie and Anne went into effect immediately. We engaged accountants, working under our auspices with the protection of work product privilege, to create books and records for the business and prepare Charlie's tax returns. This ensured that, if charges were ever laid against Charlie, their work would be protected by the confidentiality of lawyer-client privilege.

We then opened negotiations with the Agency and requested a postponement to give us time to prepare the business books and records for the audit. This was granted. The first meeting took place at our offices. As we have mentioned before, if you are the target of an audit, try to avoid meeting with the Agency on your own premises. That gives the Agency the opportunity to make judgments about you, and trap you into revealing information best kept confidential. Anne and Charlie were only too happy to have us, as their legal counsel, meet with the auditor. We provided Charlie's properly completed books and records, as well as his signed tax returns, and a revised return that we had prepared for Anne to declare previously unreported funds that she had received from the business.

The Agency took it all away to review. In due course, the Agency sent Charlie a tax assessment, which included interest and penalties, totalling nearly $180,000. Anne was also assessed for a small amount of tax, which she promptly paid off with a loan from her brother. Round One had ended successfully for our side. Now we had to reckon with the payment of the tax bill and the filing of a taxpayer relief request for removal of, or alternatively a reduction of, the penalties and interest that had been charged.

We prepared a comprehensive plan and made submissions to the CRA as to the amount Charlie would be able to pay on a monthly basis. Then, in a detailed legal brief, supported by affidavits and medical reports, we set out why Charlie had been unable to file and pay his taxes when due. We addressed the medical conditions of Charlie's family. We indicated that Charlie was now tax-compliant and wished to pay his tax debt, but was financially strapped. Because of these problems, we requested some accommodation—i.e., cancellation of penalties and interest, at minimum. Our legal brief was presented to the Agency in a format that would enable us to go to the federal court for judicial review if our request was refused.

While the Agency was considering our request for taxpayer relief, we consulted with a trustee in bankruptcy to see if Anne and Charlie could benefit from a creditor proposal. Anne's brother had agreed to loan her $40,000, and she believed she could get a second mortgage on the house for $34,000. If we discounted the interest and penalties on Charlie's tax debt, the total of unpaid tax, GST, and deductions at source was about $84,000. This would enable us to offer the Agency almost all the tax due, if it would agree to waive penalties and interest. Chances were good, we believed, that the Agency would accept this proposal. If it didn't, Charlie would be forced into bankruptcy, and the Agency would get only Charlie's fleet of trucks, which were subject to conditional sales contracts.

Of course, this procedure was not without risk. There was a slim possibility the Agency would make a grab for the family home under Section 160 of the Income Tax Act, by claiming that Charlie had been paying the mortgage even though Anne was the owner. They could take the position that his tax dollars had been diverted to pay for Anne's house. But we were prepared to argue that, since the mortgage payments were quite small and Charlie had to live somewhere, this was the equivalent of his paying rent for accommodation. In short, the position, in our view, was quite defensible. After many meetings with us to discuss the pros and cons, Charlie and Anne agreed to submit a creditor proposal. The wheels were put in motion and the hearing date was set. The only creditor to appear at the hearing was the CRA. At first, the CRA representatives refused to accept the proposal, but we countered with the stark reality that they were forcing Charlie into bankruptcy. We also told them that if they opposed discharging Charlie from bankruptcy in order to get some extra years of payments, we would counter by showing that they had earlier refused a generous proposal. The Agency usually prefers cash in hand to coming home empty-handed. They asked for time to reconsider and the creditors' meeting was adjourned for two weeks.

At the next meeting, the Agency sent in its star negotiator. He was a very large and unfriendly looking fellow, a big-city tough guy. He greeted us with, "We're not accepting your proposal unless there's a financial sweetener attached to it."

We excused ourselves for a hurried conversation in the hall with our clients. Anne called her brother to ask if he could add another $10,000 to her loan. He agreed and we went back to the Agency with a total of $84,000 on the table. That was our final offer. It was that or bankruptcy.

It was now the CRA team's turn to go outside to confer. When they came back we had a deal. The Agency agreed to waive the penalties and interest in favour of recovering the tax due.

They had saved face. Charlie had come through the audit and filings without a prosecution, and now penalties and interest had been forgiven. Charlie and Anne's business and peace of mind were saved.

This story had a happy ending—even though Charlie's tax problem truly began through a series of tax delinquencies. It's important to note that we were able to help Charlie so dramatically because he had legal protection *before* he had any conversations with the Agency. Controlling the flow of information to the Agency was the strategic advantage that helped win the day.

A Case of Critical Miscalculation

This case shows how an audit can become a lifelong nightmare.

When Larry received a notice that the Agency wanted to audit his books and records, he wasn't overly concerned. He'd been reporting all his income, remitting the GST, and filing tax returns prepared by a reputable accounting firm. He didn't see the Agency's sharp teeth until it was too late!

Here is Larry's story, in his own words, taken from a telephone interview.

"We opened up our own business in 1993. It was a contracted local-dispatch delivery service. People would call us up and we would send a vehicle and a driver to make the delivery. We charged $2.50 for each delivery. My wife and I kept 75 cents for our dispatching troubles, answering phones, and our time. The drivers kept the other $1.75. If we did 100,000 deliveries a year, times 75 cents, we made $75,000 a year. That's what we paid our GST on.

"We had our taxes done every year by one of the biggest chartered accountancy firms in Canada. Then Revenue Canada came along in 2003, did an audit on us, and told us we should be paying GST on the full $2.50 paid for each delivery. By its calculations, if we did 100,000 deliveries times $2.50, then we should be paying GST on $250,000.

"I tried to argue that my wife and I received only 75 cents per delivery. The other money never came into our hands. We never collected it and so we shouldn't pay GST on it. But the tax people said we owed GST on the $250,000 a year, and demanded that we pay arrears based on that amount. With penalties and daily interest it added up to something like $130,000. We didn't have that kind of money. We had never had that money in the first place, so how were we supposed to pay it?

"The tax people started to hound us for this ridiculous figure by sending 'Requirements to Pay' orders around town. Once people hear the Agency is coming, they get afraid. My business started to crumble around me. Then they froze my bank account, and we were out of business.

"I went back to my accountants, and they would take no responsibility. They said that they deal only with what's put in front of them and if we gave them incorrect tax information, it wasn't their problem.

"Then things started to get personal. One of the local tax people has a son who played in a hockey league with my son. He started digging around my past tax returns and started denying deductions I had made for travel expenses when I was able to do some business while away at out-of-town tournaments with my son. Our child tax benefits were withheld from us. At one point one of the tax people even came to my house. Unfortunately, I was not at home or he never would have got inside. He sat down at our table, and proceeded to tell my wife 'it looks like you guys live a pretty good life, looking at the things we had in our home, not knowing that half of the stuff on our walls was bought at garage sales.

"By now six or seven different people have handled my case at the tax office in our town. Every time somebody new gets their mitts on the file, they come at me again. Last week somebody new closed my bank accounts again.

"It's a little hard to go into some places now; it's a little harder to look people in the eye because in a small community, word gets around.

"The whole ugly picture isn't over yet. The tax people are still demanding their $130,000. It's probably more by now. But it's not like I have this money under my mattress. There's no proof that I collected this money; there's no proof that anybody paid me this money. There was no GST collected on the full $2.50 whatsoever, so I don't know why I'm being held responsible for this money. The whole thing was a mistake made by the accounting firm, and a mistake on my part in trusting its advice. In the future we would have corrected the mistake and things would have been done different, but the tax people didn't give us a chance.

"Revenue Canada is holding this over my head and will continue to do so probably for the rest of my life. Maybe if they'd left the business alone, we would have had a chance to pay them back, and make a deal with them or something. But now that they've done what they've done, there is no way in this lifetime I will ever be able to pay them back!"

At the time of writing, there was no apparent end to Larry's nightmare except a proposal of bankruptcy. Because he had waited for years before contacting us, the window of opportunity to challenge any of the Agency's assessments had expired long ago. His case was statute barred and even a court application would not be successful in reopening it. Because he believed that he had filed his business taxes accurately and responsibly, Larry thought he had nothing to fear from an audit, and he didn't seek appropriate legal help at an early enough stage. By the time he realized the danger, he was firmly caught in the Agency's jaws.

Authors' Note: We would like to offer a thought regarding the role of Larry's accounting firm. Many taxpayers, small business owners in particular, do not retain the services of an accounting firm for a formal audit of their financial statements. Instead, the taxpayer provides his or her own statements of revenues and expenses, and the accounting firm prepares the annual financial statements and the tax returns based upon the information provided. These financial statements are prefaced by a Notice to Reader to this effect. If Larry provided his revenue statements to the accounting firm without explaining the complete structure of his business, it is possible that the accounting firm would not have been aware of Larry's miscalculation.

The CRA chose to pursue Larry for the full burden of the uncollected GST, probably because it was easier to attack the source than to chase down all the drivers who should have been collecting GST from Larry and then remitting it to the CRA. If the drivers had charged Larry the GST, he would have been able to deduct it from his total revenues, which would have cancelled out the additional GST owing and kept his business intact.

11

TAX APPEALS

Filing your tax return is just the beginning of what can be a long and trying relationship with the Agency. Months after you have hit the electronic SEND button, or put the extra stamps on your oversize and overweight manila envelope and dropped it in the mailbox, you can get a nasty surprise. There, in your mailbox, quietly lurking behind the CRA logo is a time bomb that can shatter your peace of mind and possibly destroy your financial stability for years to come.

It's a reassessment notice. Hundreds upon hundreds of thousands of taxpayers each year receive some degree of reassessment. It may only be a few dollars different from what you anticipated when you completed your tax return. It may be a few hundred. Or it can be thousands! All tax returns are fed automatically into a computer for an initial review. The computer makes adjustments to your tax credits and deductions based on formulae programmed into it, and readjusts your balance owing or refund coming accordingly. Review this assessment carefully and definitely question any information that you believe to be inaccurate. This usually can be handled through a phone call to your area tax office supported by a letter or fax.

These assessments are so common that it's a sure bet every taxpayer will encounter one at some point during their taxpaying lifetime.

But this first reassessment may not be the end of it.

LETTER FROM A BELEAGUERED TAXPAYER

I do both my wife's and my taxes (QuickTax) each year. Both my wife and I are retired and in our early 60s. A few months later we would get a notice accepting our tax returns and our money and then later in the year, my wife or I would get another notice that—oops—Rev Can found an error and we owe more money. We would write a cheque and two to three months later we would get a thank-you letter and a $0.00 balance due. A short period later, we would get another notice ordering us to pay another few thousand dollars more because of an error on our part. So we would send off another cheque and then we would receive another thank-you letter and another $0.00 balance. This rotation could occur several times during a tax year. When I would phone Revenue Canada each time to discuss each and every notice, I would be told they have the right to check returns over and over and over ad infinitum. It gets terribly tiring and frustrating and maddening that Rev Canada can keep doing this to everyone in Canada. Our frustration level is ongoing and very upsetting.

You must be very wary if, some months after you have filed your tax return, the Agency comes back with more questions or requests for receipts. It may mean that after a careful review of your tax return, with human involvement—and possibly as the result of a secret lifestyle assessment, or in response to a "snitch call"—it has been decided that your tax return or returns have not been accepted as an accurate representation of your taxable income and thus you have not paid sufficient tax. They can send you a revised tax bill, with the addition of daily interest and penalties. All amounts are payable immediately.

Taxpayers are as shocked by the result of a reassessment as they are by an audit. The reassessed total of tax due and payable can be devastatingly large—possibly enough to spell financial ruin.

Devastating or not, you must do something. The tax bill rendered is due, and will remain due, until such time as the Agency, or eventually a tax court judge, agrees to reduce the balance. As we discussed in chapter seven, if you don't pay, the Agency could take everything.

Before you consider selling the house, the car, the cottage, and the kids, there is an option: the tax appeal process. You may choose to undertake this on your own, or retain the services of a tax lawyer. Either way you should understand the process and requirements for filing a tax appeal.

FILING A TAX APPEAL: AN OVERVIEW

Internal Appeal: The Notice of Objection

The first thing to do is to be sure that you understand the income tax rules as they apply to your situation. Sometimes these rules seem unfair, no matter how correctly the Agency is applying them. When the rules are clear, then no matter how much you dislike paying more tax, there may be no choice. If you think you have good reasons to debate the assessment, contact your area tax service office and request an adjustment. Sometimes this works.

If you are not prepared to accept the assessment, you must file a formal notice of dispute, called a Notice of Objection, before 90 days elapse from the date of mailing of the Notice of Assessment or Reassessment to which you are objecting. The date showing on the Notice of Assessment is presumed to be the date of mailing.

Even if you think you have a verbal agreement of settlement with the Agency, file the Notice of Objection if the 90-day deadline is fast approaching and a correcting reassessment has not yet been issued. The Agency's verbal promises to correct an assessment are not binding. Get it in writing.

To assist taxpayers with the process, the CRA provides an outline for a Notice of Objection. You can download it online, fill it in, and even submit it online. You'll find the form on the CRA website at *www.cra-arc.gc.ca/E/pbg/tf/t400a*.

While you have the option to send this notice by email, we recommend you always send your Notice of Objection by registered mail as well.

Once your Notice of Objection is filed, an appeals officer will review the case. This tax official is supposed to give your case a "fresh review." The appeals officer is required by the Agency's administrative policy to give you a copy of the original auditor's working papers. You will have to ask for them, but do insist and don't take no for an answer.

You may wish to arrange a meeting with the appeals officer. In person, you may convince the officer that your position is correct. If you would rather not meet face to face, make your case in writing. If the appeals officer agrees with you, the reassessment will be "varied" (and a new reassessment issued). If not, the reassessment will be "confirmed." This exhausts the routes of administrative appeal within the Agency and now you must give up and pay up. Or you can resort to the tax court.

Appealing to the Tax Court of Canada

You have the right to file an appeal to the tax court within 90 days of the mailing date of the tax agency's decision rejecting your Notice of Objection. This involves filing a Notice of Appeal.

There are two procedures available for this: the Informal Procedure and the General Procedure. The Informal Procedure is most often used by taxpayers wishing to represent themselves in tax court because it minimizes the legal steps involved in the appeal process.

For income tax appeals, the Informal Procedure is limited to cases in which the amount of federal tax and penalties in dispute for each taxation year, excluding interest, is $12,000 or less. For GST appeals, on the other hand, there is no limit to the amount in dispute.

Ninety percent of taxpayer disputes are resolved before reaching the Tax Court of Canada (excluding CPP/EI disputes). The majority of decisions appealed to the tax court are resolved *in favour of the CRA.*

When the amount in dispute in an income tax case is greater than $12,000, a taxpayer who wishes to choose the Informal Procedure must limit the amount under appeal to $12,000; otherwise your appeal to the tax court must follow the General Procedure.

The Tax Court of Canada provides an outline for taxpayers to follow when filing an appeal. For the Informal Procedure, you can submit a detailed letter, but you are encouraged to use the Tax Court of Canada's online submission form. Go to *www.tcc-cci.gc.ca/main_e.htm* and click on the "Submit Online Documents" option on the bottom-left corner. You will be guided through an online form where you can fill in the fields and even attach documents relevant to your appeal.

For the General Procedure, you must submit a form, which can be downloaded at *www.tcc-cci.gc.ca/rules/gen/formule21(1)a_e.htm.* You will also find a comprehensive guide to the procedures for filing your appeal.

If the situation is at all complicated, if the total owing is staggering, or if there is any possibility that the review that resulted in the reassessment may lead to a criminal investigation, you would be wise to seek the assistance of a tax lawyer rather than try to manage it yourself.

Always Send Your Notice of Appeal by Registered Mail
Once your Notice of Appeal has been duly filed, you will receive notice that you have been set down for trial. You may be directed to a pretrial hearing conference.

Pretrial Hearing Conference

This takes place after an appeal has been set down for hearing. Then the court may direct the parties (you and the Agency's legal counsel) to appear before a judge for a pre-hearing conference to consider
- the possibility of settlement of any or all of the issues in the appeal
- appropriate means to simplify the issues and to shorten the hearing
- the possibility of obtaining admissions of fact or documents
- the advisability of amending the pleadings or defining the questions in dispute
- any other relevant matter

At this hearing, each party should provide the court with a brief that
- reveals the theory of the party's case
- indicates the facts the party intends to prove at trial, and the evidence that will be led
- outlines the propositions of law the party will rely on, and the authorities identifying particular passages in support of them

If you can come to a settlement with the Agency at this stage, it will shorten the process considerably. Otherwise, you will have to prepare for your day in court.

An important caveat before you decide to take on the Agency in court:
Since your appeal is in challenge of an assessment, the onus rests upon
the taxpayer to establish the facts upon which it should be varied
or upset. If this is not possible, the taxpayer loses. This is called the
reverse onus of proof. If you are daunted by the prospect of having to
prove the Agency wrong, it's best not to start down this road on your
own. An experienced tax lawyer can help you navigate through what
can end up being a complex process.

**As tax lawyers, here's how we would normally approach a tax
appeal:**
The law gives taxpayers the right to file a Notice of Objection by registered mail within 90 days of the mailing date of the reassessment.
This is simply a statement that you do not agree with the reassessment, along with the reasons, and notice to the Agency that you are
prepared to present evidence to prove your objection. This temporar-
ily stops the clock on collection action, although daily interest will
continue to accrue as long as the tax is unpaid. If you win your appeal,
that interest will be cancelled.

We ensure that the Notice of Objection is filed by registered mail
within the 90-day window. Then we move into the work of disproving
the Agency's assessments.

If the figures are at issue, we start by reviewing the matter with
accountants—yours if you prefer, or another retained by us and protected through our lawyer-client privilege—to get their opinion about
how the Agency's assessors have proceeded and where they have made
accounting errors, if any. It is important to look at everything through
the lens of impartiality, especially since taxpayers can be very emotional because they feel that they have been victimized by the Agency.
Often, we find that the CRA reassessment has been based on incorrect
assumptions. Part of the assessment will undoubtedly be correct, but
we can often leverage the flaws to challenge the Agency's decision.

When we are properly prepared, we will try to negotiate a reasonable settlement with the Agency. Unfortunately, the CRA's attitude often is "we have done our work and will stand behind it. If you don't like it, you can always appeal to the tax court."

And so we can. First, however, our client must decide whether or not the amounts of money in issue outweigh the expense of an appeal to the tax court. Trials take time to prepare for and attend, making the process costly for the taxpayer. On the other hand, the Agency doesn't have to worry about costs and will fight to the death using the unlimited resources of the Government of Canada. These are your tax dollars at work. (If the taxpayer decides to stand down at this stage, but does not have the funds to pay the tax bill right away, we have other options to approach the Agency to request reductions in interest and penalties, arrange payment schedules, and more.)

Due to the lengthy period of time it takes a case to proceed through the tax court and even, perhaps, through an appeal to the federal court, we recommend that a taxpayer pay the tax to stop the interest-clock running. This is because the CRA typically charges approximately 4% above the bank prime rate, and if the matter drags on for a few years, the interest expenses themselves can be quite formidable. Paying the tax does not mean that you accept the Agency's position. If your case is successful, they will have to repay the tax you paid with interest.

12

WHEN THE TAX COLLECTOR COMES

 Taxpayers can negotiate manageable solutions to their tax debt, enabling them to resolve the situation and get on with their lives.

After the amnesty, after the audit, after the assessment, after the appeal—or quite simply after the filing of your tax return on time, in complete honesty, with all the receipts and income statements required—there will come the time of reckoning, when the Agency must be paid its due.

When the Agency comes knocking at your door, what do you do if you don't have the means to settle the tax debt—in full or in part? In this section we offer some guidelines on how to deal with the Agency when tax is due and sufficient funds are not at hand.

THE AGENCY'S OFFICIAL POSITION TOWARD TAXES OWING

The Agency has an obligation to fairly apply the provisions of the Income Tax Act and other tax acts. It must ensure that all taxpayers pay the required amount of tax, duties, fees, and penalties due to the Crown.

Tax is due in full by the balance-due date. For individuals, this is April 30. For corporations, this is two or three months after the end of the corporation's tax year. Unpaid tax balances accrue daily interest from that date, and the interest will accumulate until such time as the debt is paid in full. If penalties also apply, these will also accrue daily interest. A tax bill left unpaid over time quickly escalates to astronomical proportions. It is in your best interest to borrow funds or even sell assets to discharge your tax debt sooner rather than later. The Agency, however, might lull you into thinking it has forgotten all about the debt by not contacting you for months on end, sometimes even years. Don't be fooled. This is its way of turning a small unpaid tax liability into what could become a financial windfall for the government. If you let the tax debt continue unpaid, the Agency will eventually take matters into its own hands, forcing you to face the consequences.

WHAT HAPPENS WHEN YOU DON'T PAY THE AGENCY?

Under the Income Tax Act, when taxes remain unpaid, interest and penalties are charged at the prescribed rate on all amounts owing, regardless of whether they are disputed or not. The longer your taxes remain unpaid, the higher the ultimate total of your debt.

The Agency won't sit back while the tax and interest adds up. It will come after you aggressively for payment. Business tax credits, GST/HST credits, EI, or CPP benefits—they can all be gobbled up by the Agency to pay your tax debt.

If there are reasonable grounds to believe that the collection of all or part of the tax will be jeopardized if there is a delay in collecting it, the Agency has the authority to take immediate collection action, including seizure of assets, garnisheeing wages, and other measures deemed necessary. These steps can be taken even before an assessment is issued, to ensure you have no warning, thus preventing you from taking steps to minimize the assets available for seizure. No application to the courts is required for any of these actions, and you will not be notified in advance.

Under the Income Tax Act or Part IX (GST) of the Excise Tax Act, if you owe tax and you transfer property to

- a spouse or a person, who has since become your spouse
- a person under 18 years of age
- a person with whom you were not dealing at arm's length

the person to whom you transferred the property becomes liable for the lesser of the amount you owe, or the excess of the fair market value of the property over the consideration given for the property.

These rules do not apply to a transfer of property between a taxpayer and his or her spouse under a decree, order, or judgment of a court, or under a written separation agreement where, at the time of transfer, the taxpayer and his or her spouse were separated and living apart as a result of the breakdown of their marriage or common-law relationship.

The Agency can hold the directors of a corporation jointly and individually liable for the payment of taxes if the corporation fails to deduct, withhold, or remit amounts deemed to be held in trust, such as GST/HST and tax deductions at source. In addition, the directors are jointly and individually liable, along with the corporation, to pay any penalty or interest that has accrued or will accrue on such outstanding amounts.

Like any creditor, the Agency will resort to legal action to recover the taxes, penalties, and interest owing to the Crown. Normally it will call into play one or more of these legal options:

- Garnishment of your wages
- Third-party demands on your customers
- Set-off of government funds due to you such as GST/HST tax

credits, income tax refunds, old age security, Canada Pension
Plan, etc.

- Seizure and sale of your assets or goods, including your bank
  accounts and other financial holdings
- Registration of a lien against your real property

As we have mentioned before, the Agency can take any of these
actions against you without notifying you in advance. Once the Agency
takes the route of garnishment, liens, and writs of seizure, it is difficult
to have these removed or withdrawn until such time as the tax debt
has been discharged. It is possible to negotiate removal/withdrawal
based upon undue financial hardship or in return for a partial payment or acceptance of an approved repayment schedule, depending on
your circumstances.

If a proactive role is taken early enough, it is frequently possible to
prevent the CRA from filing liens against your real property. A tax lien
can wreak havoc when filed against your house. If you own other real
property, a lien will also be registered against it, too. The Agency can
attack all property you now own, or will acquire in the future (including through inheritance, etc.). However, it is possible to negotiate to
have a lien withdrawn if this will permit you to leverage your equity
in the property (through sale or borrowing) to access funds to pay
off—or at least pay down—the tax.

If you are more than 30 days late with a payment as negotiated by a payment proposal with
the CRA, the Agency will likely freeze your bank
accounts until payment of the full tax debt is
received, or an advocate (tax lawyer or other)
renegotiates a payment arrangement. This action
can be taken without notifying you in advance.

TAX COLLECTION SCENARIOS: WHAT TO DO IF THIS HAPPENS TO YOU

The Agency Has Frozen My Bank Accounts

This is one example of a third-party demand, and you must fix the situation immediately. The bank is required by law to freeze your account on demand and send your money to the Agency. Imagine . . . all your money, just gone! Afterwards you may be unable to make your mortgage payments or to pay utilities and other bills, making a bad problem worse.

If you receive a third-party demand, contact a tax lawyer immediately to take action to protect you and work on your behalf to secure a postponement.

If successful in putting a postponement in place, the lawyer then should begin to negotiate with the Agency to agree upon a better way to settle your tax debt.

THE AGENCY AND JOINT BANK ACCOUNTS

Q: *You allege the CRA can freeze or seize or garnish one's bank account. Is this possible without a warrant or court order? And can this be done when the account is jointly owned?*

A: The short answer is *yes*. Even if the account is jointly owned, the CRA can seize it. The joint owner who does not owe the tax will have to prove how much of the money belonged to him or her and request release of those funds. This would be a very difficult and intricate negotiation, and you would be well advised to retain the services of an experienced tax lawyer.

The Agency Has Garnished My Paycheque

When the Agency garnishes your pay, your employer is required to send the requested portion of each paycheque—usually a substantial part—directly to the Agency, often leaving you without enough money to live on.

Contact your advocate (tax lawyer, preferably) right away, because time is of the essence. Depending upon your individual circumstances, it may be necessary to either file an offer to settle your debt, or arrange an installment agreement you can live with.

The Agency Sent Demand to Pay Letters to My Customers

If you're a small business owner or independent contractor who is behind on your taxes, these letters are an effective way for the Agency to get its money. Not only does your cash flow dry up, but now your customers, by virtue of receiving the Demand to Pay requirements, are informed that you're a tax deadbeat.

The first priority is to negotiate a release or postponement of the third-party Demand to Pay. It's necessary to become tax compliant and begin negotiating a favourable settlement while attempting to persuade the tax Agency to stop its business-killing tactics.

WHEN YOU REALLY CANNOT PAY THE TAX

The Income Tax Act gives the Agency the authority to take extreme action to collect on tax owing. However, there are provisions under which taxpayers can negotiate manageable solutions to their tax debt, enabling them to resolve the situation and get on with their lives.

Our tax law firm uses a lawyer-protected tax relief negotiation to help reach an equitable settlement with the Agency when, because of extraordinary circumstances, taxpayers are unable to meet their tax obligations.

Here are the principal ways in which lawyer-managed negotiations can help taxpayers seek equitable tax relief:

Payment Arrangements

The CRA will consider alternative payment arrangements when the taxpayer has tried all reasonable ways to get the necessary funds and still cannot pay the amount due. In this situation, a mutually satisfactory payment arrangement based on the taxpayer's ability to pay has to be worked out. When determining ability to pay, the Agency expects the taxpayer to make a full financial disclosure and give tangible evidence of income, expenses, assets, and liabilities. Collections officers will verify the information provided before accepting an arrangement. However, if the tax debt stays outstanding with no mutually acceptable payment arrangement, the Agency can take legal action such as garnisheeing income or directing a sheriff to seize and sell assets.

WHAT IF I OWE SALES TAXES?

Q: *I owe the CRA for non-remitted sales tax and the penalties that were assessed. Can I negotiate them lower? My business had a downturn due to the new smoking by-law, SARS, and the hockey strike.*

A: Both the provincial retail sales tax and the GST are trust monies, and therefore the principal amount owing cannot be reduced. Since government legislation caused

> the problem that created your business downturn, it may be possible to negotiate to have penalties and interest removed citing your inability to pay. This would be a very tough sell and you likely would need the assistance of a very deft and experienced tax lawyer.

Taxpayer Relief Provisions

Section 220(3.1) of the Income Tax Act gives the Agency discretionary power to waive or cancel interest or penalties on a tax debt. It is supposed to apply where a taxpayer has not been able to meet his obligations to pay because of extraordinary circumstances beyond his control. These include

- natural or man-made disasters, such as a flood or fire
- civil disturbances or disruptions in service, such as a postal strike
- serious illness or accident, or serious emotional or mental distress (e.g., death in the immediate family), stress, depression, habitual drunkenness, or drug abuse

The Agency can also forgive penalties and interest when they result primarily from the actions of the Agency. These include

- processing delays that result in a taxpayer not being informed, within a reasonable time, that an amount was owed
- errors in CRA publications or incorrect information provided to taxpayers
- delays in providing information, such as when a taxpayer is unable to make a payment because the necessary information was not made available
- processing errors that result in a taxpayer being unaware of certain obligations

The Agency may also forgive interest when taxpayers cannot pay amounts owing because of circumstances beyond their control. For example:

- if collection of the tax debt has been suspended because of an inability to pay caused by the loss of employment and the taxpayer is experiencing real financial hardship
- when a taxpayer is unable to conclude a reasonable payment arrangement because the interest charges absorb a significant portion of the payments

In this situation, an equitable settlement might be negotiated whereby the tax authorities would waive all or part of the interest for the period from when payments commence until the amounts owing are paid provided agreed-upon payments are made on time.

Your history of compliance or non-compliance will be a factor in obtaining such relief. Those who, over the years, have made a habit of non-payment may have some difficulty in convincing the Agency to forgive interest and penalties.

A Hypothetical Taxpayer Relief Application Scenario

Assume that, because of pressing personal problems, you have failed to file your tax returns for three or four years. Life was hard. You were in a high-stress situation, and had family problems. Then comes a telephone call or letter from the CRA asking why you haven't filed.

In panic mode, you rush over to your accountant and have the returns prepared and filed. A month or so later comes a reassessment with huge penalties and a letter from the Agency saying that the matter is being reviewed by its Compliance department. What does this mean?

It could be that criminal prosecution is being contemplated, in addition to your reassessment. But before this possibility materializes, you have to deal with the huge civil penalties that have been levied. A call to the CRA nets the reply "Why don't you ask for taxpayer relief?"

Sounds simple doesn't it? Really, it is just a way for that particular bureaucrat to get rid of you.

Your accountant says he or she can handle it and sends off a letter to the Agency giving a few reasons why you deserve taxpayer relief. You hear nothing for several months. Then comes a new letter from the Agency. Your request has been refused.

About 75% to 80% of such requests are refused. Why? For the most part, the request for tax relief has been presented in the form of a letter or memo without substantive supporting evidence. There is nothing in this type of submission to force the Agency to pay attention to it. So it's very easy to stamp it denied.

What can make the difference between acceptance and denial of your request for tax relief is a formal legal submission. Such a submission is designed from the outset to be taken before a Federal Court judge for judicial review of the bureaucrat's decision should your request be denied.

About 75% to 80% of requests for taxpayer relief are refused. Why? For the most part, the request for tax relief has been presented in the form of a letter or memo without substantive supporting evidence.

Your Situation from the Agency's Point of View

From the outset, the Agency is your adversary. Its objective is to get what it considers to be the proper mix of tax, penalty, and interest out of you and then, if it can also build a substantive case against you, proceed to prosecution. The Agency is not your friend and it will do you no favours. Where's the percentage in that?

This is not to imply that tax officials are evil or will purposefully try to "put you under." Most of the individuals working in the CRA try to fulfill their work mandate as fairly as possible. However, they must enforce tax compliance—that is their job. Nevertheless, some CRA employees will go to extreme lengths to collect taxes, and in the process, the lives and families of taxpayers can be badly disrupted or destroyed.

We are aware of at least one instance of a non-filer who, because of huge penalties and the relentless pursuit of the Agency, actually committed suicide. He simply could not continue to handle the pressure. Tragically, his situation most likely could have been resolved through a legal submission for tax relief.

When seeking taxpayer relief, the Agency must be approached in a serious, legal manner, through legal channels, in order to ascertain that all your rights are protected.

THE CASE OF THE NAIVE RESTAURATEUR

Carolyn owned a small restaurant. She went through a nasty divorce. Her ex failed to pay alimony, and she was barely able to support the children on her income from the restaurant. Putting food on the table was a priority. Taxes took a back seat. She coped by not filing her returns for her income or the GST.

One day a tax official came in to her restaurant to follow up on why she wasn't filing. Carolyn was almost hysterical with fear. She told the official her story, which he seemed to accept, because that day he went away. But the problem didn't go away, and a few months later Carolyn received an assessment. She found a way to pay a small part of the tax, but the rest of the tax debt, with daily interest, continued to accumulate as the years passed.

At this stage, we believe it would have been possible to negotiate a taxpayer relief settlement on Carolyn's behalf. We would have argued that she had few assets, children to raise, and no extra cash, and made a taxpayer relief application for reduction or removal of penalties and interest.

Unfortunately, Carolyn tried to negotiate a deal with the tax collectors herself. She was unaware of the formal processes for taxpayer relief, and her attempts were unsuccessful. All the same, the Agency didn't harass her for the money, and as the years went by she became less and less fearful. Then Carolyn met Jim and, after a time, they married. They bought a house together. They were happy, but Carolyn was still worried about that unpaid tax bill.

She knew the CRA had not forgotten about her because she kept receiving statements. With penalties and daily interest, the total was now well over $50,000!

The hammer fell one day when a letter from Collections demanded payment in full. Carolyn's assets were at risk and she didn't know what to do. That's when she came to us.

It was too late on a number of fronts to make a taxpayer relief application. Purchasing a house, which had by now increased substantially in value, had given her the means to pay off the tax debt. Had we been retained before the property purchase, we could have negotiated the penalties and interest down to a level that Carolyn could pay. We might also have negotiated a payment schedule to allow Carolyn to space repayment out over time. Her mistake was trying to do it herself.

Most taxpayers with tax debts make the same mistake. Here's why: the tax collector's response, when the taxpayer says he or she has no money to pay, is to claim that there is money, and the taxpayer has used it for something else—to buy a house, perhaps, take a holiday, or feed the children. The Agency's underlying philosophy is that the tax-evader has been using the peoples' money, and now the people want it back. Either give it back voluntarily or the Government will take it from you forcibly.

Carolyn tried to negotiate with these tough tax collectors herself. Then her financial circumstances changed for the better. The Agency was lying in wait, and struck when she was most vulnerable.

The bottom line: waiting too long to seek taxpayer relief can be dangerous.

A tax lawyer can prepare the appropriate legal brief, complete with supporting documentation, and insist that the matter receive proper review. By proceeding in this manner, your tax lawyer serves notice on the Agency that the matter can be taken to the federal court for judicial review. Just this fact is enough to concentrate the attention of the Agency and obtain the best possible result for the client. This is not to say the bureaucrat will cave in, but merely underlines that, if possible in the circumstances, every legal and reasonable accommodation will be extended by the CRA. Why would the Agency do otherwise when, if it denies the request too easily, a judge will be reviewing the criteria upon which a tax relief decision was rendered? In fact, if the courts slap down a CRA employee too often, it will reflect poorly on his performance evaluations!

Most importantly of all, the tax lawyer will be able to protect your financial information through the privilege of lawyer-client confidentiality, revealing to the Agency no more than is necessary to support your appeal. Remember, in a failure-to-file situation, prosecution is always a distinct possibility. Retaining legal counsel—a.k.a. legal protection—at the outset of your dealings with the Agency can make a critical difference later should you find yourself in criminal court.

THE CASE OF THE RETIRING DENTIST

Robert was a well-respected dentist with a successful practice. Now he was finally ready to retire. Unfortunately, years before, Robert had listened to a financial adviser and invested in some bad tax shelters. The CRA disallowed the deductions he had taken, and for almost 10 years an ongoing tax court battle had been in progress, with a law firm representing the group of investors. In the meantime, daily interest on the tax debt kept clicking away.

After several years of still-unresolved litigation, Robert came to us for an opinion on his chances of ultimate success. We assessed his case and gave him our opinion that it was highly unlikely the group of investors would win their suit against the CRA. Knowing that his current amount due to the Agency had already become huge and unmanageable, and would grow even larger as he waited for the outcome of the lawsuit, Robert asked us to negotiate a settlement with the CRA on his behalf. After lengthy negotiations, which included a creditor proposal, we were able to settle with the Agency by having it forgive the penalties and interest (which was 58% of the total amount owing).

The bottom line: Because Robert sought the help of an experienced tax lawyer while he was still in a position to negotiate, he was able to retire with his finances reasonably intact.

EQUITY FINANCING

Whatever the outcome of your request for taxpayer relief, you will, in all but the most unusual and extenuating of circumstances, still have a tax bill to pay. Our advice is always to pay this off as quickly as you can. This may require borrowing money from family, from colleagues, or if possible, from a financial institution.

Banks traditionally shy away from helping borrowers with tax problems. Any collateral or home equity a taxpayer may pledge as security against the loan is, from a bank's perspective, at risk since the Agency may end up seizing the asset. This is especially true if you try to negotiate a larger mortgage or a second mortgage when the Agency has already placed a lien against your home.

Any equity you have, in your home or in other assets, should be leveraged to help you discharge your tax debt. When traditional lenders will not assist you, you will need to negotiate an equity loan through other venues. Alternative lenders may be more willing to advance funds when they know that a lawyer-negotiated tax settlement will be the outcome of the situation. Once the tax debt is paid, the lien can be lifted from the property, assuaging the lender's discomfort to a large extent.

BANKRUPTCY

Filing for bankruptcy should be your last resort. It may not be necessary, particularly if appropriate equity financing can be arranged and a tax settlement negotiated.

Bankruptcy follows you for a long time. If a potential employer knows of the bankruptcy, you may not get the job. It could take years to rebuild your credit status. If you are in the market for a home, mortgage, credit card, or automobile, you'll be charged higher interest rates assuming credit is even extended.

For some people, however, bankruptcy may be the only—and therefore the right—choice. But first, ask yourself: Can I live with the consequences? Don't file for bankruptcy just because you are tired of hearing from the tax collector.

Even more importantly, don't choose bankruptcy because the "nice" tax collector has suggested that you "just make a bankruptcy proposal." For a bureaucrat, bankruptcy can be a great solution. It gets your case off his books and he can show results, albeit negative. But what appears an easy answer on the surface can put you in jeopardy.

Here's how the Agency's game can play out. Assume that a tax debtor, hounded to his wit's end by the Agency, submits a creditor proposal to finally be free. Most normal creditors will vote in favour of a proposal based on higher yields for them. After all, this is only good business. The Agency, however, can afford to reject the proposal regardless of the yield. The Agency is not, after all, a business. It is a bureaucracy and a tax collector! And the Agency itself is also often the largest creditor, and as such is in a position to be the deciding factor in the acceptance or rejection of the creditor proposal. And rejecting the proposal affords the Agency an opportunity to make more money down the road. Here's how:

Let's say the creditor proposal is for over $75,000 in debts. This makes it, at the time of writing, a Division I proposal, which means that if the proposal is refused, the debtor automatically goes bankrupt. The Agency's refusal to accept the proposal will push the tax debtor into bankruptcy. As a bankrupt, the debtor initially appears to pay a reduced amount of tax in a bankruptcy, and will become eligible for discharge after nine months. This is a huge improvement over the many more months it would have taken him or her to pay out the terms of the creditor proposal.

Attractive as this scenario appears, there is huge catch. Just as the tax debtor is coming up to the end of nine months as a bankrupt, the Agency steps up and opposes the debtor's discharge, seeking a conditional order from the Court for additional payments. This adds years to the bankruptcy before the court will grant a discharge. At this stage, the debtor, still a bankrupt, is completely helpless, and has no financial power to make decisions. He or she remains trapped in tax hell, despite the agony of the bankruptcy.

Alternate Choices

It can be wiser for a tax debtor to develop, with the help of an experienced tax lawyer, a strategic plan to make a creditor proposal under the Bankruptcy Act.

A properly planned proposal can provide the framework under which a debtor's financial obligations may be restructured, with the consent of a majority of the creditors, and without the debtor having to go bankrupt.

There are two types of proposals—Division I and Division II.

Division I Proposals are classified as having aggregate debts above $75,000. These proposals must be passed by special resolution, meaning a majority in number and two-thirds in value of the unsecured creditors' proven claims. If a Division I Proposal is rejected, the debtor is bankrupt automatically.

Division II, or Consumer Proposals, are classified as having aggregate debts less than $75,000, or in the case of a joint filing, under $112,500. This is excluding any debts secured by the person's principal residence, such as a mortgage. Consumer Proposals are passed by ordinary resolution, which is 50% plus 1 in value of unsecured creditors' proven claims. If creditors reject a Division II Consumer Proposal, the debtor is left in the same position as before he or she attempted the proposal, and need not go into bankruptcy.

Why Work with a Tax Lawyer on a Proposal?

When the Agency is the largest creditor, a tax lawyer can play an important role in helping you safely navigate your way to financial resolution if you decide to make a proposal under the Bankruptcy Act. A Trustee in Bankruptcy cannot work as your exclusive advocate, and might actually harm your negotiating position. The trustee also represents your creditors, and is placed in a situation where a conflict of interest can arise easily.

Iain Ramsay, Professor of Law, Osgoode Hall Law School, York University, Toronto, said it best:

> The trustee in bankruptcy is the representative of creditors, and also adviser and counselor to a debtor. Trustees advertise their services widely to debtors in the Yellow Pages. The trustee is clearly in potential conflicts of interest and in my study of trustees I conclude that the relationship of trustee to debtor is one of professional dominance by the trustee.

Your tax lawyer acts only for you and will be fully loyal to your interests. The trustee will have to advise your creditors what you tell him or her about your assets, perhaps to your detriment. Speaking to a trustee is like talking into the Agency's ear.

Moreover, your lawyer has the privilege of lawyer-client confidentiality. The lawyer must be truthful when negotiating your settlement, but will be in control of the timing of how and when to provide that information. This can be a strategic advantage.

The Dangers in a Bankruptcy

Filing for bankruptcy will not protect you from the consequences of your tax filing behaviour. If an investigation shows that you are not declaring all your revenue (i.e., if tax evasion was involved) or if a large lifestyle assessment is levied against you, a criminal charge can be laid against you for tax evasion. Thumbing your nose at the government by going bankrupt can lead them to want to make an example of you and start a criminal prosecution. If you are convicted, the judge will impose a fine. If you are bankrupt and cannot pay, jail time is usually the result.

Your tax lawyer will deal with this possibility as part of his submission for equitable relief and try to stop potential prosecution. His or her legal training and tax knowledge, with the protection of lawyer-client confidentiality, will help in working out a beneficial tax settlement for you.

THE CASE OF THE EVANGELICAL BANKRUPTS

Here's a case where two senior citizens in Saskatchewan tried to use a combination of bankruptcy and religious doctrine to avoid paying more than $205,000 in outstanding income tax. The debt was a result of questionable investments the couple had made that generated significant tax consequences.

In a letter to a representative of the creditor (the CRA), objecting to their bankruptcy discharge, the couple alleged that

> as bonded servants in the life of Jesus Christ in the kingdom of God Almighty...His saving grace has redeemed us from the charge of any debt as a debtor to any claim.... We are not debtors and do not deal in debt to discharge matters as that would be serving another master, the debtor (SATAN).

When scheduled to appear before the Registrar in Bankruptcy, the couple had ill-advisedly retained a non-lawyer to represent them, unaware that this individual was under an injunction by the Law Society of Saskatchewan that prevented him from practising at the bar of any court of civil or criminal jurisdiction in the province. When the Registrar in Bankruptcy refused to allow this advocate to appear on the couple's behalf, they were forced to represent themselves against a most formidable opponent—the CRA—who, as the creditor, was opposing an early discharge of bankruptcy in the hope of securing more payments over a longer term. (We discussed this same danger earlier, on page 187.)

The couple had offered the CRA a promissory note in lieu of payment of their tax debt because "as citizens of Canada, we are entitled to a pro-rated share of the value of Canada, which can be set off against the alleged debt owing."

Unimpressed by the combination of religious zeal and patriotic rhetoric, the Registrar in Bankruptcy ruled in favour of the CRA, granting conditional discharge from bankruptcy to each spouse upon payment of a set amount over a period of three years, along with a suspended discharge to ensure compliance with the filing and payment of income tax during those years. Given that the ideal situation is unconditional discharge at the end of nine months, this ruling was a serious financial blow to the couple.

The Trustee in Bankruptcy's notes indicated that the bankruptcy filing was tax-driven and that the couple had chosen not to pursue their right under the tax act to appeal.

The moral of the story: Neither God nor bankruptcy can stay the hand of the CRA.

SOME ASSETS THAT ARE PROTECTED FROM THE AGENCY

In rare cases, assets may be exempt from seizure. These include certain pensions, locked-in RRSPs, and some RRSP funds that are classified as annuities under an insurance policy. Here's a list of what likely can be protected from the Agency—or any other creditor.

Segregated Funds

Segregated funds are essentially life-insurance contracts that invest your principal in mutual funds and guarantee a return of at least 75% of your principal at the end of the contract period. Should you die, your beneficiary receives the guaranteed amount or the cash value of the fund, whichever is greater. Because the segregated funds are considered insurance, your money is secure from creditors, unless the segregated funds were purchased when you owed money to the Agency or other large creditor. If taxes were due at that time, Section 160 of the Income Tax Act can kick in and the funds may be open to seizure.

Universal Life Insurance

A universal life insurance policy is a creditor-proof way to ensure you are protected in the event of illness or death. It's also a tool for building your retirement funds without increasing your tax bill. When you purchase a universal life policy, you pay more than the cost of the insurance. After the premium and management fees are deducted, the remainder goes into a tax-sheltered investment fund of your choice. When you retire, you can withdraw funds or name your lender as beneficiary and then borrow money against the policy to supplement your retirement. Upon death, the policy repays the loan and interest, and the balance is paid to secondary beneficiaries.

ASSET PROTECTION—ONSHORE AND OFFSHORE

Often people seek ways to legally protect their property from potential third-party claims. Sometimes they put assets in a non-revocable trust for the benefit of themselves and their family. For this to work, proper timing is essential. Asset protection must be implemented well before tax and other debts actually arise.

A Canadian resident can settle (i.e., set up) such a trust in an offshore jurisdiction. This can make it much more difficult for future third-party creditors to seize the trust's assets. The effectiveness of the trust is enhanced if the assets are not situated in Canada, and the persons who have power to order a distribution of the trust funds should not live here.

Even an offshore trust may not entirely "bullet proof" trust assets from third-party creditors, but, if properly set up, it will be difficult for creditors to access the assets of the trust.

According to the Auditor General's report to Parliament in February 2007, the CRA had identified 72 trusts by 2005—with capital gains of over $600 million—that had been created to avoid paying tax to the Canadian government. These trusts were reassessed, and the Agency's Appeals Branch upheld the reassessments. Since then, some taxpayers have settled with the agency and unwound the trusts; others are appealing the decisions further.

SUCCESS AND FAILURE OF ASSET-PROTECTION PLANS

The success of an asset-protection plan depends upon many factors. Creditor-proofing plans are more effective if they are implemented when there is no existing problem, when the client is solvent, and when there is no expectation of a claim that may render the client insolvent.

On the other side of the coin, there are a wide variety of remedies to assist creditors' attempts to acquire the assets of a person who is on the eve of, or is already in, financial distress. These include the Assignments and Preferences Act, Bankruptcy and Insolvency Act, Fraudulent Conveyances Act, Bulk Sales Act, Absconding Debtors Act, and the Income Tax Act.

Those who could try to challenge an asset-protection plan include
- the CRA
- secured creditors
- provincial revenue authorities
- preferred creditors

As noted previously, the Agency has rights under Section 160 of the Income Tax Act. These include attacks on conveyances of property from a taxpayer to non-arm's-length persons, spouses, or common-law partners.

GAMBLING WITH THE TAXMAN

Sometimes you can roll the dice and win an appeal.

For four years, Brian and Terry LeBlanc, two brothers—unmarried and in their 30s—lived together. They spent the time just sitting around their house in Aylmer, Quebec, drinking beer, watching television, and buying large numbers of sports lottery tickets on Pro-Line, Point Spread, and Over/Under—always multiples of long-shot game scores. Whenever they won, they ploughed everything back into buying still more tickets. By 1996, they were buying up to $300,000 worth of tickets a week, about $10 million to $13 million of them a year.

They calculated they won only about 5% of the time, but the pot was always huge because of the long-shot game scores they picked. Over a four-year period, they bought about $55 million in tickets and came out making about $5 million profit.

They were like the Mackenzie brothers (Bob and Doug)—just two guys living alone, eating pizza, and swilling beer, with no visible means of support other than their lottery winnings.

In Canada, lottery winnings are not considered taxable income. However, if gambling is your only source of income, then it can be argued that gambling is your business, and therefore the income earned as a result is subject to tax.

The LeBlanc brothers eventually attracted the attention of the CRA for this very reason. The CRA wanted a share of their remarkable winnings, on the grounds that they must have had a system if they were making so much money, and having a system made it a business.

In this case, the CRA lost its gamble.

D. G. H. Bowman, Chief Justice of the Tax Court of Canada, decided that the brothers didn't owe any income taxes. They were just lucky compulsive gamblers, he ruled. They did not have a system. Maybe they had a purchasing pattern, but no system, and their lucky purchasing of winning tickets did not constitute a business where skill and risk management is required. There is no skill in buying a winning lottery ticket. It is a game of chance. It's not like a pool hustler winning money at pool where skill with the cue is required.

The turning point in their case came from a defence witness, gambling expert Dr. Garry Smith. He testified the odds of winning in sports lotteries the way the brothers did are "astronomical" and that "skill plays no part in winning at sports lotteries."

The judge compared them to a Las Vegas gambler placing large stacks of chips all over the roulette table for one spin of the wheel. That is not indicative of anything other than a tendency to bet heavily, he wrote, not of a system designed to provide a business income. Nor are they like the racehorse owner with access to insider information on trainers, the health of the horses, and the track conditions on which to base his wagers. "Rather they are more accurately described as compulsive gamblers, continually trying their luck at a game of chance," the judge said, and ruled in their favour.

Sometimes, in an appeal, the taxpayer just comes up lucky. But what are the odds?

13

PARTING THOUGHTS

I certify that the information given on this return and in any documents attached is correct, complete, and fully discloses all my income.

Sign here _____

It is a serious offence to make a false return.

Telephone 555-555-1212   Date 04/30/2007

Once your tax return has been completed, signed, and sent off to the tax office with a cheque for the balance owing enclosed, you, along with most taxpayers, hope this is the end of it.

This would be nice, but unfortunately, it's just not the case. Your signature on your tax return commits you to an ongoing relationship with the CRA that can end in reassessment, audit, investigation, and even criminal prosecution.

It's the only relationship that transcends death. After all, your estate must file a final tax return with the Agency, and that return can be dragged through reassessment, audit, and investigation, too.

And if you don't handle the filing of your return responsibly—in a timely manner and with complete honesty—it may become a living death that destroys you financially, emotionally, and socially.

If we were to assign the CRA a motto, it would undoubtedly be *Taxare ut nihil* (taxation or nothing).

In the same spirit, we offer all taxpayers the following words to live by: *Protegum tuum pugum* (cover your ass).

Forewarned is forearmed.

SOURCES

Pages 13–14: Audit programming staffing figures: *Report of the Auditor General of Canada*, Exhibit 5.1, March 2004.

Page 14: CRA Corporate Business Plan Priorities (for the years 2007–2008 to 2009–2010): Canada Revenue Agency *Summary of the Corporate Business Plan, 2007–2008 to 2009–2010.*

Page 15: Ibid.

Page 20: "The Minister of National Revenue...CRA Service Complaints program": Canada Revenue Agency, "Taxpayers' Ombudsman: Overview," *www.cra-arc.gc.ca/agency/ombudsman.*

Page 21: "It's tempting to dismiss. . . 'user-friendly'": Jonathan Chevreau, *Financial Post*, May 29, 2007.

Page 23: Desert island cartoon: *www.grahamharrop.com.*

Page 25: "A Slight Mistake": case study based on an article in the *Ottawa Citizen*, June 1, 2007.

Pages 43–44: "Vancouver Resident Fined. . ." and "Compliance Program Helps. . . ": case studies adapted from a CRA Media Room postings, using information obtained from court records, *www.cra.gc.ca/convictions*.

Pages 44–45: "Couple Jailed in Tax Evasion Case": Tony Van Alphen, *Toronto Star*, May 1, 2007, C1.

Page 47: Oscar Wilde, "Letter to an English Tax Collector," April 1889.

Page 57: "Building-Trade Perils" data: *Will You Do It for Cash?*, Canada Revenue Agency, RC4406. p. 4.

Pages 66–68: "The Case of the Non-Filing Consultant": case study adapted from a CRA Media Room posting, *www.cra.gc.ca/convictions*.

Page 94: "Half of the 700,000 . . . in 2001": "Ontario Moves Against Companies That Don't File Tax Returns," CBC News (online), February 10, 2003, *www.cbc.ca/money/story/2003/02/10/ecker030210*.

Page 100: "Without solicitor-client privilege . . . advise themselves": J.C. McRuer, Royal Commission Inquiry into Civil Rights.

Page 111: "The Voluntary...prosecution": Canada Revenue Agency, *www.cra-arc.gc.ca/agency/investigations/vdp-e.html*.

Page 135: "Section 238(1)" and "Section 239(1)": Income Tax Act, Canada Revenue Agency *Summary of Corporate Business Plan, 2005–2006 to 2007–2008*, March 2005.

Page 190–191: "The Case of the Evangelical Bankrupts": includes information from an article by Deana Driver, *Lawyer's Weekly*, May 4, 2007.

ACKNOWLEDGEMENTS

We are deeply appreciative of the assistance a number of people have given in the preparation of this book.

Patricia Brownridge Plant, an outstanding communicator, brought her considerable talents to the organization and clarification of the material that forms the basis of this book.

Barbara Hopkinson, Brad Wilson, and Noelle Zitzer, our editors, were of great help with their comments and suggestions.

Many thanks to Brigitte DioGuardi, a tax lawyer and our colleague, for her insightful comments, and to Joyce Bruno, our legal assistant, for her work in transcribing and correcting the text. We also are grateful to our friends and colleagues who offered comments, corrections, and suggestions. Please accept our heartfelt thanks for your generous assistance.

Of course, any errors or omissions in this book, which we have tried to make very straightforward and readable, belong to the authors alone. For these, we proffer to you, kind reader, our *mea culpa*.

AUTHORS' NOTE

In this book we have shared some real-life tax stories from our case files. We are always interested in adding to our understanding of the dilemmas real-life taxpayers face in the course of their relationship with the CRA.

If you have a "Tale from Tax Hell," or simply one of frustration, that you would like to share with us, for possible inclusion in future writings, we invite you to send us your story. Feel free to substitute aliases in place of real names and/or adapt identifying details.

Email your stories to *TaxStories@taxrx.ca*. Or mail them to

DioGuardi Tax Law, LLP
5090 Explorer Drive, Suite 510
Mississauga, ON L4W 4T9
Attn: Tax Stories

INDEX

A

accountants
  accredited, 31
  auditing of financial state-
    ments, 160–63
  lack training to negotiate
    amnesty, 114
  required to cooperate with
    CRA, 33, 87–89, 100–104,
    111–12, 126
  unaccredited, 30–31
  when not to let them talk to
    CRA, 106–8
"aggressive" accounting, 14, 30
Agnew, Spiro, 3
amnesty, 8, 105–30. *See also*
  Voluntary Disclosures
  Program (VDP)

best negotiated by a tax
  lawyer, 105–6, 114,
  128–30, 158–59
CRA's ability to repudiate, 130
frequently asked questions,
  113–15
more often sought by women,
  121
why necessary, 115–28
appeals, 12, 32–33, 164–71
filing, 166–71
how tax lawyers handle them,
  170–71
arbitrary audits. *See* lifestyle
  audits
assets
  foreign, 87

required to cooperate with
CRA, 6, 7, 17, 33–34, 91,
95–96, 126, 147
required to cooperate with
IRS, 38
BDO Dunwoody, 100–101
Black, Conrad, 4
Bowman, D.G.H., 195–96
building trades, 56–58
business expenses, 140, 147–48

C
Canada Revenue Agency (CRA)
ability to oppose discharge of
bankruptcy, 92–93, 187
ability to repudiate amnesty,
130
business priorities, 14–16, 18
Canadians' perception of, 4,
18
as collection agency, 5–6, 17,
20, 91, 93–94, 154–55,
170, 173–77
collection tactics, 81–99,
173–75
Compliance Programs. See
"tax police"
International Tax Group,
38–39, 117, 125–26
matching program, 24–27,
56–57, 70–72, 139–40

no time limit on ability to
reassess, 31, 85, 132
powers of enforcement,
17–18, 21–22, 135
powers of investigation, 5–6,
7, 134–36
presumption of guilt, 2, 15,
17–18, 144
questionnaires as traps,
150–51
relationship with Revenue
Quebec, 38, 93–94
statistics, 13–14
strategies for dealing with,
97–98
time limit on tax debts, 90–92
verbal agreements not binding, 8, 60, 128
when not to let accountant
talk to, 106–8
when not to talk to on your
own, 107–8
Who's Who, 11–12
capital gains, on real estate,
75–76, 124–25
Capone, Al, 2–3
cash, payment in, 58, 61–62,
64, 140, 148
Certified General Accountants
(CGAs), 31
Certified Management Accountants (CMAs), 31

foreign assets, 87, 147, 152
foreign pensions, 72–73, 124

G
gambling, 194–95
garnishment, 90–92, 174–75,
    176–77
general contractors, 56–58
Goods and Services Tax (GST),
    14, 32, 48–49, 57–58,
    65–66, 94, 152–53, 168,
    174, 178–79
governments, taxing power, 21
gratuities, 59–60
"grey" accounting, 14, 30

H
Harmonized Sales Tax (HST),
    14, 48–49, 57–58, 65,
    152–53, 178–79
Hatch, Richard, 4
Helmsley, Leona, 3
hobby businesses, 48–49, 74–75
homeowners, pitfalls of paying
    contractors in cash, 58
home-renovation businesses,
    56–58
homes
    business use, 52, 74–75
    flipping, 75–77

liens against, 6, 11–12, 155,
    175, 186
protecting from CRA, 86–87
renovation, 56–58, 76–77
renting out, 70–72, 124–25
seizure by CRA, 21–22, 121,
    150, 186
transfer to spouse, 85–86,
    145–46
hotel employees, 59–60
housekeepers, 61–66

I
income
    failing to report, 120–27,
        140, 147
    from gambling, 194–96
    from hobbies, 48–49, 74–75
    from illegal activities, 87,
        95–96
    misrepresentation, 5, 101
    offshore, 36, 38–39, 101
income splitting, 54–55
Income Tax Act
    Section 150, 80
    Section 160, 85, 122, 159
    Section 162, 80
    Section 220, 179
    Section 231, 100–101, 135
    Section 238, 16, 118, 135
    Section 239, 16, 135